KAIMOKUSHŌ
OR
LIBERATION FROM BLINDNESS

BDK English Tripiṭaka 104-IV

KAIMOKUSHŌ
OR
LIBERATION FROM BLINDNESS

by

Nichiren

Translated from the Japanese
(Taishō Volume 84, Number 2689)

by

MURANO Senchū

Numata Center
for Buddhist Translation and Research
2000

First Printing, 2000
ISBN: 1-886439-12-5
Library of Congress Catalog Card Number: 99-74476

Published by
Numata Center for Buddhist Translation and Research
2620 Warring Street
Berkeley, California 94704

Printed in the United States of America

A Message on the Publication of the English Tripiṭaka

The Buddhist canon is said to contain eighty-four thousand different teachings. I believe that this is because the Buddha's basic approach was to prescribe a different treatment for every spiritual ailment, much as a doctor prescribes a different medicine for every medical ailment. Thus his teachings were always appropriate for the particular suffering individual and for the time at which the teaching was given, and over the ages not one of his prescriptions has failed to relieve the suffering to which it was addressed.

Ever since the Buddha's Great Demise over twenty-five hundred years ago, his message of wisdom and compassion has spread throughout the world. Yet no one has ever attempted to translate the entire Buddhist canon into English throughout the history of Japan. It is my greatest wish to see this done and to make the translations available to the many English-speaking people who have never had the opportunity to learn about the Buddha's teachings.

Of course, it would be impossible to translate all of the Buddha's eighty-four thousand teachings in a few years. I have, therefore, had one hundred thirty-nine of the scriptural texts in the prodigious Taishō edition of the Chinese Buddhist canon selected for inclusion in the First Series of this translation project.

It is in the nature of this undertaking that the results are bound to be criticized. Nonetheless, I am convinced that unless someone takes it upon himself or herself to initiate this project, it will never be done. At the same time, I hope that an improved, revised edition will appear in the future.

It is most gratifying that, thanks to the efforts of more than a hundred Buddhist scholars from the East and the West, this monumental project has finally gotten off the ground. May the rays of the Wisdom of the Compassionate One reach each and every person in the world.

NUMATA Yehan
Founder of the English
Tripiṭaka Project

August 7, 1991

Editorial Foreword

In January 1982, Dr. NUMATA Yehan, the founder of the Bukkyō Dendō Kyōkai (Society for the Promotion of Buddhism), decided to begin the monumental task of translating the complete Taishō edition of the Chinese Tripiṭaka (Buddhist canon) into the English language. Under his leadership, a special preparatory committee was organized in April 1982. By July of the same year, the Translation Committee of the English Tripiṭaka was officially convened.

The initial Committee consisted of the following members: (late) HANAYAMA Shōyū (Chairperson); BANDŌ Shōjun; ISHIGAMI Zennō; KAMATA Shigeo; KANAOKA Shūyū; MAYEDA Sengaku; NARA Yasuaki; SAYEKI Shinkō; (late) SHIOIRI Ryōtatsu; TAMARU Noriyoshi; (late) TAMURA Kwansei; URYŪZU Ryūshin; and YUYAMA Akira. Assistant members of the Committee were as follows: KANAZAWA Atsushi; WATANABE Shōgo; Rolf Giebel of New Zealand; and Rudy Smet of Belgium.

After holding planning meetings on a monthly basis, the Committee selected one hundred thirty-nine texts for the First Series of translations, an estimated one hundred printed volumes in all. The texts selected are not necessarily limited to those originally written in India but also include works written or composed in China and Japan. While the publication of the First Series proceeds, the texts for the Second Series will be selected from among the remaining works; this process will continue until all the texts, in Japanese as well as in Chinese, have been published.

Frankly speaking, it will take perhaps one hundred years or more to accomplish the English translation of the complete Chinese and Japanese texts, for they consist of thousands of works. Nevertheless, as Dr. NUMATA wished, it is the sincere hope of the Committee that this project will continue unto completion, even after all its present members have passed away.

It must be mentioned here that the final object of this project is not academic fulfillment but the transmission of the teaching of the

Buddha to the whole world in order to create harmony and peace among humankind. To that end, the translators have been asked to minimize the use of explanatory notes of the kind that are indispensable in academic texts, so that the attention of general readers will not be unduly distracted from the primary text. Also, a glossary of selected terms is appended to aid in understanding the text.

To my great regret, however, Dr. NUMATA passed away on May 5, 1994, at the age of ninety-seven, entrusting his son, Mr. NUMATA Toshihide, with the continuation and completion of the Translation Project. The Committee also lost its able and devoted Chairperson, Professor HANAYAMA Shōyū, on June 16, 1995, at the age of sixty-three. After these severe blows, the Committee elected me, Vice President of Musashino Women's College, to be the Chair in October 1995. The Committee has renewed its determination to carry out the noble intention of Dr. NUMATA, under the leadership of Mr. NUMATA Toshihide.

The present members of the Committee are MAYEDA Sengaku (Chairperson); BANDŌ Shōjun; ISHIGAMI Zennō; ICHISHIMA Shōshin; KAMATA Shigeo; KANAOKA Shūyū; NARA Yasuaki; SAYEKI Shinkō; TAMARU Noriyoshi; URYŪZU Ryūshin; and YUYAMA Akira. Assistant members are WATANABE Shōgo and UEDA Noboru.

The Numata Center for Buddhist Translation and Research was established in November 1984, in Berkeley, California, U.S.A., to assist in the publication of the BDK English Tripiṭaka First Series. In December 1991, the Publication Committee was organized at the Numata Center, with Professor Philip Yampolsky as the Chairperson. To our sorrow, Professor Yampolsky passed away in July 1996, but thankfully Dr. Kenneth Inada is continuing the work as Chairperson. This text is the twentieth volume to be published and distributed by the Numata Center. All of the remaining texts will be published under the supervision of this Committee, in close cooperation with the Translation Committee in Tokyo.

MAYEDA Sengaku
Chairperson
Translation Committee of
the BDK English Tripiṭaka

June 28, 1999

Publisher's Foreword

The Publication Committee works in close cooperation with the Editorial Committee of the BDK English Tripiṭaka in Tokyo, Japan. Since December 1991, it has operated from the Numata Center for Buddhist Translation and Research in Berkeley, California. Its principal mission is to oversee and facilitate the publication in English of selected texts from the one hundred-volume Taishō Edition of the Chinese Tripiṭaka, along with a few major influential Japanese Buddhist texts not in the Tripiṭaka. The list of selected texts is conveniently appended at the end of each volume. In the text itself, the Taishō Edition page and column designations are provided in the margins.

The Committee is committed to the task of publishing clear, readable English texts. It honors the deep faith, spirit, and concern of the late Reverend Doctor NUMATA Yehan to disseminate Buddhist teachings throughout the world.

In July 1996, the Committee unfortunately lost its valued Chairperson, Dr. Philip Yampolsky, who was a stalwart leader, trusted friend, and esteemed colleague. We follow in his shadow. In February 1997, I was appointed to guide the Committee in his place.

The Committee is charged with the normal duties of a publishing firm—general editing, formatting, copyediting, proofreading, indexing, and checking linguistic fidelity. The Committee members are Diane Ames, Eisho Nasu, Koh Nishiike, and the president and director of the Numata Center, Reverend Kiyoshi S. Yamashita.

Kenneth K. Inada
Chairperson
Publication Committee

June 28, 1999

Contents

A Message on the Publication of the English Tripiṭaka
NUMATA Yehan v

Editorial Foreword *MAYEDA Sengaku* vii

Publisher's Foreword *Kenneth K. Inada* ix

Translator's Introduction *MURANO Senchū* 1

Notes on Transliteration 3

Kaimokushō or Liberation from Blindness

Chapter I
The *Saddharmapuṇḍarīka-sūtra* 7

Chapter II
Am I Not the Practitioner of the *Saddharmapuṇḍarīka-sūtra*? 41

Chapter III
The Five Testimonies to the Truthfulness of My Faith 79

Chapter IV
The Age of Degeneration 95

Chapter V
Die a Martyr for the Cause of *Saddharmapuṇḍarīka-sūtra*! 111

Glossary 127

Bibliography 131

Index 133

A List of the Volumes of the BDK English Tripiṭaka (First Series)

Translator's Introduction

The *Kaimokushō* was written by Nichiren (1222–1282) in 1272. *Kaimoku* literally means "to open the eyes." Here the title is rendered as *Liberation from Blindness,* in order to avoid a different connotation, "to stare with astonishment."

Nichiren was arrested by the Kamakura government on the twelfth day of the ninth month of 1271 and was sentenced to exile on Sado Island. When Nichiren's troop escort arrived at Tatsunokuchi execution ground that night, the war minister NAGASAKI Yoritsuna, who was preparing to issue a mobilization order the following day to repulse the Mongolian invasion, attempted to behead Nichiren, whom the nervous minister regarded as the most powerful religious dissident defying government policy for the control of the nation. His illegal action was, however, suspended by the Regent, and Nichiren was sent to Sado as had been officially ordered. Nichiren arrived at the island at the beginning of the eleventh month of the year, was detained at Tsukahara for six months, and then was moved to Ichinosawa, where he stayed until he was released in March 1274.

After he was arrested in 1271, many of his followers left him. The followers of other Buddhist sects rejoiced at the government's disposal of the head of the Daimoku faith and, further, wished to see him annihilated. The people of Sado Island were no exception. Possible assassins were loitering about his house of detention day and night. Nichiren realized that he could be killed at any time. Yet he was not frightened but glad to see this because he thought that if he dedicated himself to the *Lotus Sutra* (the *Saddharmapuṇḍarīka-sūtra*), he would be able to expiate the sins that he had committed in his previous existences and have great happiness in his next life. He was ready to die a martyr for the cause of the *Lotus Sutra.*

However, what was more important to him than this determination he held for himself was how to persuade his followers to follow his example. To pray to the gods was useless, he thought. He wrote in Chapter V, "If the gods could protect the keeper of the right teachings of the Buddha, why were Maudgalyāyana and Siṁha killed?" (The *Kaimokushō* was not originally divided into chapters or sections; the division of the text into five chapters has been arbitrarily done by the translator.)

The only way to have his followers keep their faith in the *Lotus Sutra* and die as martyrs for its cause was to tell them that the wonderful Dharma of the *Lotus Sutra* was the only way to Buddhahood. In order to explain this to them, he began by criticizing religions other than Buddhism, and then Buddhist sutras other than the *Lotus Sutra*. This is translated as Chapter I.

But Nichiren suddenly changed the subject and concentrated on the direct and vital question: "Am I not the practitioner of the *Lotus Sutra*?" This is presented as Chapter II. To practice a sutra means to act according to the teachings expounded in it. He spent more pages on this chapter than on any other. In order to answer this question, he quoted the five testimonies to the truthfulness of his faith in the *Lotus Sutra* given in Chapter III.

In Chapter IV, Nichiren followed Miao-le and established the three kinds of arrogant people, following Chapter XIII of the *Lotus Sutra*. According to the wording of the *Mahāparinirvāṇa-sūtra,* he identified those three kinds of arrogant people with the three kinds of enemies of the *Lotus Sutra*.

Nichiren wrote the *Kaimokushō* in his exile at Tsukahara in the second month of 1272. He had very few reference books and a poor supply of paper, pens, and ink. He was motivated to write to his few remaining followers as soon as possible in order to transmit this thought and faith to them before he might be killed. This sense of urgency resulted in making the *Kaimokushō* the longest work ever written by Nichiren.

The *Kaimokushō* was addressed to Shijō Kingo, who was the representative of the followers of Nichiren in the Kamakura District.

Notes on Transliteration

1. The Chinese pronunciation is given to Chinese proper names, except the titles of some books (see Note 2). The Japanese pronunciation corresponding to the Chinese is given in parentheses only when the Chinese proper name is used for the first time in this translation.

2. The Japanese pronunciation is given to:

a. The titles of the sutras and *śāstra*s whose Sanskrit originals are not known. The Chinese pronunciation corresponding to the Japanese is given in parentheses only when the title appears for the first time in this translation.

b. The titles of Chinese Buddhist books. The Chinese corresponding to the Japanese is given in parentheses only when the title appears for the first time in this translation.

3. Sankō, Gotei, *sangen,* and *gojō* are rendered as the three Huang emperors (Kō emperors), the five Ti emperors (Tei emperors), the three truths (*hsüan, gen*), and the five virtues (*ch'ang, jō*), respectively. Tenson (Heavenly Venerables), Genki (Original Ether), *jingi* (humanity and justice), and *reigaku* (rituals and music) are translated into English; the Chinese is given first, the Japanese second in parentheses.

4. *Kō* (filial piety) and *chū* (loyalty to one's lord) are given in Japanese with the Chinese in parentheses to clarify the meaning of the respective sentences. *Kōkyō* (*Book of Filial Piety*) is translated into English; the Japanese is given first, the Chinese second in parentheses.

5. *Hokekyō* is always expressed in Sanskrit: *Saddharma-puṇḍarīka-sūtra*. When the three different Chinese texts of the sutra are referred to, the Sanskrit title is replaced by: *Myōhōrenge-kyō* (*Miao-fa-lien-hua-ching*); *Shōhoke-kyō* (*Cheng-fa-hua-ching*); or *Tembon-myōhōrenge-kyō* (*T'ien-p'in-miao-fa-lien-hua-ching*).

6. The names of the following sects are explained in parentheses only when they appear for the first time in this translation: Hossō (Dharmalakṣaṇa) Sect, Jōjitsu (Satyasiddhi) Sect, Kegon (Avataṁsaka) Sect, Kusha (Kośa) Sect, Ritsu (Vinaya) Sect, Sanron (Three Śāstras) Sect, Tendai (T'ien-t'ai) Sect, Tendai Hokke (T'ien-t'ai Saddharmapuṇḍarīka) Sect, Yuishiki (Vijñaptimātra) Sect.

7. The Sanskrit originals of some proper names in sutras and *śāstras* are not known to us. Those proper names are translated into English. The quotations from the *Saddharmapuṇḍarīka-sūtra* are taken from Senchū Murano's English translation of the *Lotus Sutra,* where the proper names whose Sanskrit originals are known are also translated into English. This is according to the policy of the translation committee that proper names translated into Chinese should be translated into English. As the result, quotations from the *Lotus Sutra* sometimes include proper names whose Sanskrit originals are translated into English.

8. Bracketed words or phrases indicate insertions by the translator that are not part of the original text.

9. The number in the outside margin indicates the corresponding page number of the Taishō Tripiṭaka.

KAIMOKUSHŌ
OR
LIBERATION FROM BLINDNESS

by

Nichiren

Chapter I

The *Saddharmapuṇḍarīka-sūtra*

Confucianism

All the people of the world should respect three kinds of persons: 208b17
lords, teachers, and parents. They should study three [religions]: Confucianism, Brahmanism, and Buddhism.

According to Confucianism, [in ancient China] there lived the emperors and kings called the three Huang emperors (Kō emperors), the five Ti emperors (Tei emperors), and the three kings. They were revered as T'ien-tsun (Tenson) or Heavenly Venerables. They were rulers of their subjects, and bridges to provide people with roadways. The people who lived before the time of the three Huang emperors were like birds and beasts because they did not know their fathers. The people who lived in the time of the five Ti emperors and after that knew their fathers. They served their parents respectfully. Ch'ung-hua (Chōka) paid respect to his father, who was notorious for his bigotry. P'ei-kung (Haidō) genuflected before his father even after he became the [first] emperor [of the Han (Kan) dynasty]. King Wu-wang (Bu-ō) [of the Chou (Shū) dynasty] made a wooden image of his [deceased] father, Shi-po (Seihaku), for worship. Ting-lan (Teiran) carved a wooden statue of his [deceased] mother also for worship. All these people were paragons of filial piety.

Pi-kan (Hikan) was beheaded by his lord, King Chou [Chou-wang
(Chū-ō)] of the Yin (In) dynasty, when he remonstrated with the 208c
monarch for fear that the country would be destroyed [because of

the king's tyranny]. Kung-yin (Kō-in), [who failed to save his lord] I-kung (Ikō), killed himself by cutting open his abdomen, pulling out the liver from his lord's body, and thrusting it into his own body. All these people were paragons of loyalty to their lord.

Yin-shou (Inju) was the teacher of King Yao-wang (Gyō-ō); Wu-ch'eng (Musei), that of King Shun-wang (Shun-ō); T'ai-kung-wang (Taikōbō), that of King Wen-wang (Bun-ō); and Lao-tzu (Rōshi), that of Confucius. These teachers were called the Four Saints. The Heavenly Venerables bowed to them. People joined their hands together before them.

These saints wrote many books compiled into more than three thousand volumes altogether, including the Three *Fen* (*Fun*), the Five *Tien* (*Ten*), and the Three *Shih* (*Shi*). Their teachings can be summarized, however, into only three *hsüan* (*gen*), or truths. The first truth is that everything exists. This truth was established by Chou-kung (Shūkō) and others. The second truth is that nothing exists. This was held by Lao-tzu and others. The third truth is that everything exists while nothing exists. This was taught by Chuang-tzu (Sōshi).

Confucians say that *hsüan* means black. Some of them say that our previous existence comes from Yüan-ch'i (Genki) or the Original Ether. Some hold that the difference between noble and humble, sorrow and joy, right and wrong, gain and loss, and so on, are just natural happenings not due to any human artificiality. Their statements are thoughtful, but it seems that they know nothing about their previous or future lives. They say that *hsüan* is black and dark, and that, therefore, it is called *hsüan*. It appears that they know only their present lives.

[The Four Saints] established the virtues of humanity (*jen, jin*) and justice (*i, gi*). According to them, when we practice these virtues in our present lives, we shall be protected and the peace of our country will be maintained, and if we do not observe them our clans and families will be ruined. They may be called saints as far as their teachings for our present lives are concerned, but they cannot be called saints when we see that they know nothing about our previous or future lives. They are not different from ordinary men who cannot look at their backs or blind men who cannot see even their fronts.

Confucians say that the person who governs his household well, serves his parents devotedly, and practices the five virtues [including humanity and justice] in his present life will be respected by his fellow workers, praised by the people of his country, appointed as a vassal by a clever king, elected to be the teacher of the king, or enthroned under the protection of the gods. They say that the fact that King Wu-wang of the Chou dynasty was served by the Five Elders, and the fact that the Emperor Kuang-wu-ti (Kōbutei) of the Later Han dynasty was protected by the twenty-eight generals, who were reincarnations of the twenty-eight constellations, are good examples showing the results of practicing the five virtues.

But they are not true saints because they do not know the past and future. They cannot save the future lives of their parents, lords, and teachers. Therefore, we can say that they do not 209a
know the favors given to them by their seniors.

Confucius knew this and said, "There is no saint in this country. There lives a person called Buddha in the west. He is a saint." He regarded Confucianism as a preliminary to Buddhism. In order to have people understand more easily the meaning of the [three] Buddhist disciplines—precepts, meditation, and wisdom—Confucius taught them rituals (*li, rei*), music (*yüeh, gaku*), and so on. By his teaching, the subjects of a king were able to understand who were noble and who were not; children were able to know that their filial piety was virtuous; and pupils were able to realize that their teachers were dependable.

Miao-le Ta-shih (Myōraku Daishi) says:

> Buddhism has been propagated in this country [without much difficulty] because Confucianism had already been taught here. Rituals and music were taught first. Then came the True Way.

T'ien-t'ai (Tendai) says:

> It says in the *Suvarṇaprabhāsa-sūtra,* "All good teachings of the secular world come from this sutra. Those who know the teachings of the secular world well should be considered to have already understood the teachings of the Buddha."

According to the *Makashikan* (*Mo-ho-chih-kuan*), [the Buddha says,] "I will dispatch three saints to China in order to teach the people there." It says in the *Shikan-guketsu* (*Chih-kuan-hung-chüeh*):

> It says in the *Shōjō-hōgyō-kyō* (*Ch'ing-ching-fa-hsing-ching*), "Moonlight Bodhisattva was called Yen-hui (Gankai) in that country; Light-Pure Bodhisattva, Chung-ni (Chūji); and Kāśyapa Bodhisattva, Lao-tzu." People of India call this country of China "that country."

Brahmanism

The second [religion to be studied is Brahmanism]. According to the Brahmanism of India, the two gods Maheśvara and Viṣṇu are regarded as the compassionate parents, gods, and lords of all living beings. Maheśvara has three eyes and eight arms.

The three persons Kapila, Ulūka, and Ṛṣabha are called the Three Seers. They lived about eight centuries before the time of the Buddha. They expounded the Four Vedas composed in sixty thousand storehouses.

At the time of the Buddha, there were six schools in Brahmanism. They studied the Four Vedas and became the teachers of the kings of the five districts of India.

After the time of the Buddha, the six schools were divided into ninety-five or ninety-six schools. Every one of these schools was so arrogant as to think that the banner of that school was higher than the highest heaven. Each school stuck to its own view more persistently than gold or a stone keeps its hardness. But their views were incomparably more profound and meaningful than those of Confucianism. They could see not only the immediate previous lives of living beings, but also two, three, or up to seven consecutive of their previous lives, or their previous lives tracing back to eighty thousand kalpas before. They also could see their future lives for eighty thousand kalpas to come. Their views could be summarized into three headings: (1) effect exists in cause, (2) 209b effect does not exist in cause, and (3) effect exists and does not exist in cause. These three views were the ultimate teachings of Brahmanism.

The so-called good brahmans observe the five precepts and the ten good precepts, practice meditation still connected with illusions, and proceed as slowly as a measuring worm toward the highest heaven, where they think they can find the place of nirvana. But they must fall from there down to the three evil regions. None of them can stay in the highest heaven although they think that, when they reach there, they can stay there forever. They cling to the teachings of their teachers. Some of them bathe in the Ganges River three times a day in cold winter. Some pull out their hair. Some jump off a rock. Some set their bodies on fire. Some set their heads and limbs on fire. Some live naked. Some sacrifice many horses to gain bliss. Some set fire to grasses and trees. Some pay homage to all trees. They do innumerable other wrong deeds like these.

They worship their teachers as respectfully as the gods worship Śakra or as vassals bow to their emperor. But none of these brahmans, good or evil, of the ninety-five schools can get rid of birth and death. Those who serve good teachers may stay in the highest heaven for two or three lives, but eventually they must fall into the evil regions. Those who serve evil teachers will fall into the evil regions in their next lives. Brahmans should be converted to Buddhism. This is the most important thing for them.

A brahman said, "The Buddha will appear in this world a thousand years from now." Another brahman said, "The Buddha will appear in this world a hundred years from now." It says in the *Mahāparinirvāṇa-sūtra*, "All the Brahmanical texts in the world were expounded by the Buddha, not by brahmans." It says in the *Saddharmapuṇḍarīka-sūtra,* "In the presence of the people, they [my disciples] pretend to have the three poisons and wrong views. They save them with these expedients."

The Sutras Expounded before the *Saddharmapuṇḍarīka-sūtra*

The third [religion to be studied is Buddhism]. The World-honored One of Great Enlightenment is the Great Leader, the Great Eye, the Great Bridge, the Great Ship Captain, the Great Paddy Field of Merits of all living beings. Although the Four Saints of Con-
209c fucianism and the Three Seers are called saints, they are ordinary men who have not yet eliminated the three illusions. Although they are called sages, they are as ignorant as infants in that they do not know causality. How can we cross the great ocean of birth and death if we make our ship from their teachings? How can we traverse the river of the six regions by making our bridge from their teachings? Our Great Teacher eliminated the cause of birth and death, which bodhisattvas must have in the earlier stage of bodhisattvahood. Needless to say, he abolished the cause of birth and death of the living beings of the six regions. He released himself from the fundamental illusion of ignorance. Needless to say, he abolished all the other secondary illusions derived from false judgment and evil desire.

The Buddha expounded his teachings for more than fifty years from his enlightenment at the age of thirty to his *parinirvāṇa* at the age of eighty. His words are all true. Not a single word of his is false. We admit that the words of Confucius and Brahmanical saints are true because their deeds are consistent with their minds. Needless to say, the Buddha never told a lie for the past innumerable kalpas. Therefore, we can say that his more-than-fifty years' teachings are the Great Vehicle when compared with Confucianism and Brahmanism, and that his words are the true words of the Great Man. All his teachings expounded from the day of his enlightenment to the evening of his *parinirvāṇa* are true.

But the sutras containing his teachings expounded during more than fifty years, compiled in 80,000 storehouses of the Dharma, are various. There are Mahayana and Hinayana sutras, true teachings and provisional teachings, exoteric teachings and esoteric teachings. The Buddha speaks gently in some sutras, and harshly in other sutras. Some words are right while others seem to be wrong. Some views are true while other views seem to be false.

Only the *Saddharmapuṇḍarīka-sūtra* contains the correct words of the Lord Teacher, Śākyamuni, the World-honored One, and the true words of the Buddhas of the worlds of the ten quarters in the past, present, and future. The World-honored One of Great Enlightenment said that he had not revealed his true teaching during the first forty and more years of his teaching, although his teachings expounded during that period are recorded in as many sutras as there are sands in the Ganges River. He said in the *Saddharmapuṇḍarīka-sūtra,* which he expounded during his last eight years, "I will expound my true teaching," and then expounded it. Thereupon Prabhūtaratna Buddha appeared from underground and proved the truthfulness of his teachings, saying, "What you have expounded is all true."

The Buddhas who were the emanations of Śākyamuni Buddha assembled and stretched their long tongues up to the Brahma Heaven to praise him. The words of these Buddhas are as clear as the sun in the cloudless sky or as the full moon at night. Look up to heaven and believe them! Bow down to the earth and think 210a
them over!

The Buddha expounds two important teachings in this sutra. These teachings are not known to the Kusha (Kośa), Jōjitsu (Satyasiddhi), Ritsu (Vinaya), Hossō (Dharmalakṣaṇa), and Sanron (Three Śāstras) Sects. The Kegon (Avataṁsaka) and Shingon Sects took these two teachings from this sutra and made them the core of their own sects. The teaching of one mind–three thousand [which means that there are three thousand things in one mind] is expounded between the lines of the "Chapter on the Duration of the Life of the Tathāgata" in the "Discourse of the Original Buddha" of the *Saddharmapuṇḍarīka-sūtra*. Nāgārjuna and Vasubandhu knew this teaching, but did not propagate it. Our great teacher T'ien-t'ai Chih-che (Tendai Chisha) was the first person to propagate it.

In order to understand the teaching of the one mind–three thousand, we must first see the truth that the ten regions interpenetrate one another. The Hossō and Sanron Sects established eight regions, but not ten. Needless to say, they did not know that the ten regions interpenetrate one another.

The Kusha, Jōjitsu, and Ritsu Sects were founded on the Āgama sutras. These sects knew only six regions, not the other four. They said that there is only one Buddha in the worlds of the ten quarters. They did not go so far as to say that there is one Buddha in the worlds of a quarter. Furthermore, they did not say that all living beings have the Buddha-nature. They said that no one other than the Buddha had the Buddha-nature. But nowadays they say that there are Buddhas in the worlds of the ten quarters, and that all living beings have the Buddha-nature. It seems that some scholars of these sects, who appeared after the extinction of the Buddha, took these teachings from the Great Vehicle and put them into their own sects.

Confucianism and Brahmanism also took some teachings from Buddhism. Brahmanism before the appearance of the Buddha was less harmful. After the Buddha, the brahmans studied Buddhism and discovered their own faults. They thought of a device. They took the teachings of the Buddha, and put them into their sects with the effect that their wrong views became worse. They created new wrong views and distorted Buddhist teachings.

So did Confucians. The Confucians and Taoists before the introduction of Buddhism into China were as naive as infants. After Buddhism was introduced in the Later Han dynasty, controversies arose between Confucians and Buddhists. After that, Buddhism was steadily propagated. [Some Confucians and Taoists became

Buddhist priests.] Some of them violated the Buddhist precepts, quit the Buddhist priesthood, and returned to secular life. They flattered their lay supporters, and took the teachings of the Buddha into Confucianism. 210b

It says in the *Makashikan,* Volume V:

> Nowadays many evil *bhikṣus* violate the Buddhist precepts, and return to secular life. They become Taoist priests to avoid attacks by Buddhists. They expound the teachings of Chuang-tzu and Lao-tzu in order to obtain fame and gain. They appropriate the teachings of the Buddha and put them into their texts. Thus, they pull higher teachings down to the level of lower teachings, nobler teachings down to the level of poor teachings, and make the two religions equal to each other.

It says in the *Shikan-guketsu,* Volume V:

> For instance, Wei-yüan-sung (Eigensū) became a Buddhist *bhikṣu,* and caused damage to Buddhism. He violated the Buddhist precepts and returned to secular life. As a secular person, he spoiled Buddhism. He took the right teachings of the Buddha and added them to Taoist texts, which were full of wrong views. "To pull higher teachings down to the level of lower teachings" means to interpret Buddhism according to Taoism and make the right teachings of the Buddha equal to the wrong teachings of Taoism. This is nonsense. "To pull nobler teachings down to the level of poor teachings" means to become a Buddhist priest, appropriate the right teachings of the Buddha, amend their wrong teachings with them, lower the eighty thousand storehouses of the Dharma with the twelve elements to the level of the book of only five thousand words compiled in only two volumes, and expound the poor teachings of that book by using the teachings of the Buddha.

This is a comment on the previous quotations from the *Makashikan.* You should read this comment.

Some Buddhist sects also [appropriate the teachings of the other sects]. Buddhism was introduced into China in the years of Yung-p'ing (Eihei) of the Later Han dynasty. The texts of other religions yielded to those of Buddhism. The Buddhist texts, however, created three sects in South China and seven sects in North China. The controversies among them were furious. In the end, they were defeated by [T'ien-t'ai] Chih-che in the Ch'en (Chi) and Sui (Zui) dynasties. Accordingly, the priests of the ten sects stopped quarreling and resumed their mission to save people.

After that, the Hossō and Shingon Sects were introduced from India. The Kegon Sect was also introduced. Among them, the Hossō Sect was the most antagonistic to the Tendai (T'ien-t'ai) Sect. The Hossō Sect was as different from the Tendai Sect as water is from fire. But Hsüan-tsang San-tsang (Genjō Sanzō) and Ts'u-e Ta-shih (Jion Daishi) studied T'ien-t'ai's commentaries [on the *Saddharmapuṇḍarīka-sūtra*], and evidently discovered their own faults. They did not convert themselves to the Tendai Sect, but it seems that they followed T'ien-t'ai in their hearts.

The Kegon and Shingon Sects are essentially Provisional Mahayana sects based on the sutras of Provisional Mahayana Buddhism. Śubhākarasiṁha San-tsang and Vajrabodhi San-tsang of the Shingon Sect took the teaching of one mind–three thousand from the Tendai Sect and made it the core of their sects. They added mudras and mantras to that teaching, and said that their teachings were more excellent than the teachings of the Tendai Sect. Those who do not know this fact think that the teaching of one mind–three thousand was already given in the *Mahāvairocana-sūtra* introduced from India.

Ch'eng-kuan (Chōkan) of the Kegon Sect interpreted the words
210c of the *Avataṁsaka-sūtra,* "Mind is like a skillful painter," with the teaching of one mind–three thousand, which he had taken from T'ien-t'ai. No one knows this.

The six sects including the Kegon Sect were introduced in Japan before the Tendai and Shingon Sects. The Kegon, Sanron, and Hossō Sects were contradictory to one another.

Dengyō Daishi appeared in this country and not only defeated the wrong teachings of the six sects, but also found that the Shingon Sect appropriated T'ien-t'ai's philosophy based on the *Saddharmapuṇḍarīka-sūtra* and made it the core of his own sect. Dengyō Daishi criticized the six sects and the Shingon Sect by quoting entirely from sutras, not from books full of diverse opinions written by scholars of the various sects. As a result, not only the high priests of the six sects, numbering eight, twelve, fourteen, or three hundred and more, but also Kōbō Daishi were defeated in debates. All the priests of Japan followed the Tendai Sect; and all the temples of Japan, including those of the six sects and Toji Temple, were affiliated with Hieizan Enryakuji Temple. Dengyō Daishi also revealed the fact that the founders of all the sects in China followed T'ien-t'ai, and thereby they were able to release themselves from the charge of slandering the Dharma.

In the course of time, the world deteriorated, and people became too ignorant to understand the profound teachings of the Tendai Sect. As the teachings of the six or seven sects were more widely propagated, the Tendai Sect was weakened by these sects. Finally, the Tendai Sect was defeated by the Zen and Jōdo Sects. These two sects are less powerful than the six or seven sects, and are not worth noting. The laymen who supported the Tendai Sect changed their allegiance to the Zen and Jōdo Sects, and all the celebrated priests of the Tendai Sect joined those two sects to help them. The lands donated to the six or eight sects were transferred to the Zen and Jōdo Sects. Now the right teachings of the Buddha have been ignored. The gods who vowed to protect the right teachings of the Buddha, such as Tenshō Daijin, Shō Hachiman, and Sannō, have deserted this country because they are not offered the delicacy of the Dharma. Instead, devils have taken advantage of their absence. Our country is now on the verge of destruction.

The Possibility of Adherents of the Two Vehicles Attaining Buddhahood

I studied the teachings of the Buddha and found that there are
211a many differences between the Buddha's teachings expounded during the first forty and more years and those expounded during his last eight years. The most important difference, however, which is pointed out by many scholars today, and which I also agree with, is that the Buddha taught during his last years the two teachings that: (1) adherents of the two vehicles, the *pratyekabuddha* vehicle and the *śrāvaka* vehicle, can become Buddhas, and (2) Śākyamuni Buddha attained enlightenment in the remotest past.

According to the *Saddharmapuṇḍarīka-sūtra,* Śāriputra is given the name of Padmaprabha Tathāgata; Kāśyapa, Raśmiprabhāsa Tathāgata; Subhūti, Śaśiketu Tathāgata; Kātyāyana, Jāmbūnadaprabhāsa Tathāgata; Maudgalyāyana, Tamālapatracandanagandha Buddha; Pūrṇa, Dharmaprabhāsa Tathāgata; Ānanda, Sāgaravaradharabuddhivikrīḍitābhijña Buddha; Rāhula, Saptaratnapadmavikrāntagāmin Tathāgata; the five hundred or seven hundred arhats, Samantaprabhāsa Tathāgata; the two thousand *śrāvaka*s, some of whom had something more to learn while others had nothing more to learn, Ratnaketurāgata; Mahāprajāpatī, Sarvasattvapriyadarśana Tathāgata; and Yaśodharā, Raśmiśatasahasraparipūrṇadhvaja Tathāgata.

These people seem to be honored in the *Saddharmapuṇḍarīka-sūtra*, but our respect for them is lessened when we see them in the sutras expounded before the *Saddharmapuṇḍarīka-sūtra*.

Now I will explain why I say this. [As I stated previously,] the Buddha, the World-honored One, never tells a lie. Therefore, he is called Saint or the Great Man. Even in Confucianism or Brahmanism, sages, saints, or seers were called so because they did not tell lies. The Buddha excels them. Therefore, the World-honored One is called the Great Man.

This Great Man says in the *Saddharmapuṇḍarīka-sūtra:*

> I have appeared in this world for the sole purpose.... I have never expounded my true teaching.... I, the World-honored One, will expound my true teaching only after a long period of expounding expedient teachings.... I have laid aside all expedient teachings.

Prabhūtaratna Buddha proved the truthfulness of the words of Śākyamuni Buddha, and the Buddhas who emanated from Śākyamuni Buddha stretched their tongues to show their approval of the teaching of Śākyamuni Buddha. Who will doubt Śākyamuni Buddha's statement that Śāriputra will become Padmaprabha Tathāgata or that Kāśyapa will become Raśmi-prabhāsa Tathāgata?

[Since the Buddha never tells a lie,] we must say that the sutras expounded before the *Saddharmapuṇḍarīka-sūtra* are also the true words of the Buddha. But we see contradictory statements in the following [seven] quotations.

[1] It says in the *Avataṁsaka-sūtra:*

> The wisdom of the Tathāgata is like the Great Medicine King Tree. This tree does not grow and benefit itself in two places [in a hole and in water]. Adherents of the two vehicles will fall into a broad, deep hole. And those who de- 211b
> stroy the roots of good will be drowned in the water of wrong views, greed, and sensuality.

The meaning of this quotation is as follows. There is a large tree in the Himalaya Mountains. It is called "Endless Roots." It is called Great Medicine King Tree. It is the great king of all the trees in the Jambudvīpa. It is 168,000 *yojana*s tall. All the trees and grasses in the Jambudvīpa will be given flowers and fruits according to the development of the roots, branches, leaves, flowers, and fruits of this tree. This tree is likened to the Buddha-nature; and all the trees and grasses, to all living beings. However, this tree does not grow in a hole of fire and in water. The minds of the adherents of the two vehicles are compared to a hole of fire; and the minds of *icchantikas* [who have no Buddha-nature] are compared to water. These two kinds of people can never become Buddhas.

[2] It says in the *Mahāsaṁnipāta-sūtra:*

> Two kinds of people will die and never be reborn. They do not know the favors given to them by others; therefore, they cannot repay the favors. These two kinds of people are *śrāvakas* and *pratyekabuddhas*. One who falls into a deep hole cannot benefit himself or others. *Śrāvakas* and *pratyekabuddhas* are like him. They will fall into the deep hole of nirvana, and will not be able to benefit themselves or others.

The purpose of the teachings of Confucianism, expounded in the texts of more than three thousand volumes, is to emphasize the importance of two virtues: filial piety or *kō* (*hsiao*), and loyalty to one's lord or *chū* (*chung*). A loyal subject grows out of a dutiful son. Filial piety is homonymic with *kō* (*kao*), meaning "high." The virtue of filial piety is higher in value than heaven. Filial piety is also homonymic with *kō* (*hou*), meaning "thickness." The virtue of filial piety is "thicker" in value than even the crust of the earth. Saints and sages of Confucianism were dutiful to their parents in their homes. Needless to say, we students of the teachings of the Buddha should know of the favors given by others and repay them. As far as we are disciples of the Buddha, we should acknowledge the four kinds of favors and repay them.

The adherents to the two vehicles, such as Śāriputra and Kāśyapa, observed the two hundred fifty precepts and the three thousand deportments and practiced the three *dhyānas*: the *dhyāna* of the stage of taste, the *dhyāna* with illusions, and the *dhyāna* without illusions. They studied the Āgama sutras and eliminated the illusions caused by false judgment and evil desire in the triple world. It appears that they are paragons of knowing favors and repaying them. But the Buddha says that they do not
211c know the favors of their parents. Why is that?

The purpose of becoming a monk by renouncing one's family is to save one's parents. Adherents of the two vehicles think that they can emancipate themselves from suffering. It may be true, but it is very difficult for them to benefit others. They may benefit others to some extent, but they will send their parents to the world where their parents can never become Buddhas. Therefore, I say that they do not know the favors of their parents.

[3] It says in the *Vimalakīrtinirdésa-sūtra:*

> Vimalakīrti asked Mañjuśrī again, "What is the seed of the Tathāgata?"
>
> Mañjuśrī answered, "Even those who have all the illusions can have the seeds of the Tathāgata. Even those who are destined to be sent to the Hell of Incessant Suffering due to committing the five sins can aspire to Great Enlightenment.... Young man of good family! A blue lotus or a mallow cannot bloom on a plateau. It blooms only in a muddy and dirty field. [In the same manner, the adherents to the two vehicles cannot become Buddhas.] Those who have already attained arhatship and become the Deservers of Offerings cannot aspire to perfect enlightenment to attain Buddhahood, just as those who have defects in sense organs cannot enjoy the pleasures of the five senses."

The meaning of this quotation is as follows. Even if the three poisons—greed, anger, and ignorance—become the seeds of Buddhahood, even if the five sins such as patricide become the seeds of Buddhahood, even if a blue lotus blooms on a plateau, adherents of the two vehicles cannot become Buddhas. Even if evil men become Buddhas, good adherents of the two vehicles cannot become Buddhas. In the sutras of the Lesser Vehicle, evil men are blamed while good men are praised. But in this sutra, good adherents of the two vehicles are slandered while evil men are praised. It appears as if this sutra were expounded by a heretic, not by the Buddha. What is emphasized most in this sutra is, I think, that adherents of the two vehicles can never become Buddhas.

[4] It says in the *Hōdōarani-kyō* (*Fang-teng-t'o-lo-ni-ching*):

> Mañjuśrī said to Śāriputra, "Can a dead tree bloom, or not? Can the water of the river of a mountain go back to its fountainhead, or not? Can a stone which is smashed into pieces recover its original form, or not? Can a parched seed put forth a bud, or not?"
>
> Śāriputra answered, "No."
>
> Mañjuśrī said, "You say that it cannot. Then why do you ask me hopefully whether you can be assured of your attainment of Buddhahood?"

The meaning of this quotation is as follows. A dead tree cannot bloom. The running water cannot go back to its fountainhead. A
212a smashed stone cannot recover its original form. A parched seed cannot put forth a bud. The adherents of the two vehicles are also like them. Their seeds of Buddhahood are parched.

[5] It says in the *Mahāprajñāpāramitā-sūtra*:

> [Subhūti says,] "The gods can aspire to *anuttara-samyak-saṁbodhi* if they have not yet done so. Those who have become *śrāvaka*s cannot aspire to *anuttara-samyak-saṁbodhi* because they will leave the world of birth and death, and lose their chance to aspire to that."

The meaning of this quotation is as follows. Subhūti says that he will not be glad to see the adherents of the two vehicles because they cannot aspire to perfect enlightenment, but that he will be glad to see the gods because they can aspire to it.

[6] It says in the *Śūraṁgama-sūtra:*

> Those who have committed the five sins will be able to become Buddhas if they hear of the *śūraṁgama samādhi* expounded in this sutra and aspire to *anuttara-samyak-saṁbodhi*. World-honored One! The arhats who have eliminated illusions cannot practice this *samādhi* because they are like a cracked pot which cannot receive any water.

[7] It says in the *Vimalakīrtinirdeśa-sūtra:*

> Those who make offerings to you [*śrāvaka*s] cannot be called paddy fields of merits. Those who make offerings to you will fall into the three evil regions.

This quotation means that the gods and men who make offerings to saintly priests like Kāśyapa and Śāriputra will fall into the three evil regions.

I thought that these saintly priests were the eyes of gods and men and the leaders of all living beings, next in rank to the Buddha. I did not realize that the Buddha criticized them repeatedly in the presence of a great multitude of gods and men. It appears that the Buddha tried to torture his disciples to death. He criticized them even more. He said that bodhisattvas are like cow's milk while adherents of the two vehicles are like donkey's milk, that bodhisattvas are like a pot of gold while adherents of the two vehicles are like an earthware pot, and that bodhisattvas are like sunshine while adherents of the two vehicles are like the glow of a firefly.

He slandered adherents of the two vehicles not in a word or two, not for a day or two, not for a month or two, not for a year or two, not in a sutra or two, but for more than forty years in innumerable sutras in the presence of innumerable multitudes of people, without a word of leniency. Therefore, everyone knew, as is said in the proverb, "I know. You know. Heaven also knows," that adherents of the two vehicles can never become Buddhas, because everyone believed that the World-honored One never told a lie. Everyone knew this, not only a person or two, but also thousands of millions of people, gods, dragons, and *asura*s of the triple world, the people of the five districts of India, the people of the four continents, the people of the six heavens of desire, of the realms of form and the formless, and the people who came to this Sahā world from the worlds of the ten quarters, including gods, men, 212b
adherents of the two vehicles, and great bodhisattvas, heard and knew this. The people who came from the worlds of the ten quarters returned to their home worlds and told the people there what

they had heard from Śākyamuni, the World-honored One, of the Sahā world. Therefore, all the people of the worlds of the ten quarters understood that Kāśyapa, Śāriputra, and the other *śrāvaka*s can never become Buddhas, and that to make offerings to them is not recommended.

But the Buddha said in the *Saddharmapuṇḍarīka-sūtra,* which he expounded during his last eight years, that adherents of the two vehicles are able to become Buddhas. How could the great multitude of gods and men believe him? All gods and men not only rejected the *Saddharmapuṇḍarīka-sūtra* but also doubted the truthfulness of the sutras expounded before the *Saddharmapuṇḍarīka-sūtra*. Thus, all the teachings that the Buddha expounded during more than fifty years were about to be considered false. They thought, "The Buddha's statement that he has never expounded his true teaching for the past forty and more years may be false. Maybe the sutra of the last eight years is not being expounded by the Buddha, but by a devil who has transformed himself into the Buddha."

However, the Buddha ignored their doubts and announced the names of kalpas, countries, and Buddhas to be given to the *śrāvaka*s in their future lives. He announced the names of the countries where adherents of the two vehicles would be reborn, the names of the kalpas in which they would be reborn, and the number of disciples whom they would teach in their future lives. Thus, the words of the Lord Teacher Śākyamuni, the World-honored One, contradicted what he had said before. Here he committed "contradiction in one's own words." That is why brahmans laughed at the Buddha, saying, "The Buddha is a great liar." The great multitude of gods and men were astonished at the words of the Buddha, and their enthusiasm cooled. The Lord Teacher Śākyamuni, the World-honored One, was blamed by the great multitude of gods and men for his contradictory statements. He explained the reason for this in various ways, but they did not seem to understand him. He was quite at a loss what to do with them.

Thereupon Prabhūtaratna Tathāgata came from the Ratnaviśuddha world in the east, riding on a great stupa made of seven

treasures, five hundred *yojanas* tall and two hundred fifty *yojanas*
wide and deep. The stupa sprang up from underground, and appeared in the sky before the Buddha. The stupa shone as bril-
liantly as the full moon rising from the eastern mountain in the
dark night. The stupa of the seven treasures was floating in the 212c
sky, not resting on the earth, nor in the highest heaven.

Now a Brahma voice was heard from within the stupa of treasures. It says in the *Saddharmapuṇḍarīka-sūtra:*

> Thereupon a loud voice of praise was heard from within the stupa of treasures: "Excellent, excellent! You, Śākyamuni, the World-honored One, have expounded to this great multitude the *Sutra of the Lotus Flower of the Wonderful Dharma,* the Teaching of Equality, the Great Wisdom, the Dharma for Bodhisattvas, the Dharma Upheld by the Buddhas. So it is, so it is. What you, Śākyamuni, the World-honored One, have expounded is all true. . . ."
>
> Thereupon the World-honored One displayed his great supernatural powers in the presence of the multitude, which included not only many hundreds of thousands of billions of bodhisattvas, headed by Mañjuśrī, who had already lived on the ground of this Sahā world [before the arrival of the bodhisattvas from underground], but also . . . men, and nonhuman beings. He stretched out his broad and long tongue upwards until the tip of it reached the world of Brahma. Then he emitted rays of light from his pores. The Buddhas who were sitting on the lion seats under the jeweled trees of the worlds of the ten quarters also stretched out their broad and long tongues and emitted innumerable rays of light. . . .
>
> Śākyamuni Buddha, wishing to send the Buddhas his emanations, who had come from the worlds of the ten quarters, and Many Treasures Buddha back to their home worlds, said, "May the stupa of Many Treasures Buddha be where it was!"

According to the *Avataṁsaka-sūtra,* when the World-honored One of Great Enlightenment attained enlightenment, Buddhas appeared in the worlds of the ten quarters and dispatched great bodhisattvas to this world to console him. In the *Mahāprajñāpāramitā-sūtra,* Śākyamuni, the World-honored One, covered the one thousand million Sumeru worlds with his broad and long tongue, and one thousand Buddhas appeared in the worlds of the ten quarters. In the *Suvarṇaprabhāsa-sūtra,* four Buddhas appeared in the worlds of the four quarters. In the *Sukhāvatīvyūha-sūtra,* the Buddhas of the world of the six quarters covered the one thousand million Sumeru worlds with their broad and long tongues. In the *Mahāsaṁnipāta-sūtra,* the Buddhas and bodhisattvas of the worlds of the ten quarters assembled at the Great Treasure Hall.

These sutras are different from the *Saddharmapuṇḍarīka-sūtra* just as a yellow stone is different from gold, as a white cloud is from a white mountain, as ice is from a mirror of silver, or as black is from blue. But a dim-eyed, squint-eyed, one-eyed, or wrong-eyed man cannot see this difference.

The *Avataṁsaka-sūtra* has no antecedent sutra. Therefore, there is no contradictory statement of the Buddha in that sutra. No one doubted the Buddha. The *Mahāsaṁnipāta-sūtra, Mahāprajñāpāramitā-sūtra, Suvarṇaprabhāsa-sūtra,* and *Sukhāvatīvyūha-sūtra* were expounded for the purpose of criticizing adherents of the two vehicles who relied on the Hinayana sutras. In these Mahayana sutras, the Pure Worlds of the Buddhas were established in the worlds of the ten quarters in order to encourage ordinary men and bodhisattvas to be reborn there. This troubled
213a adherents of the two vehicles. There are some differences between the Hinayana sutras and the Mahayana sutras. In the Mahayana sutras, it says that the Buddhas appear in the worlds of the ten quarters; that great bodhisattvas are dispatched from the worlds of the ten quarters; that this particular sutra is expounded in the worlds of the ten quarters; that the Buddhas assembled from the worlds of the ten quarters; that Śākyamuni, the World-honored One, stretched his tongue over the one thousand million Sumeru worlds;

or that the Buddhas stretched their tongues. All these statements are given, I believe, for the purpose of criticizing the teaching of the Hinayana sutras that there is only one Buddha in the worlds of the ten quarters.

The differences between the Hinayana sutras and the Mahayana sutras are, however, not so great as the differences between the *Saddharmapuṇḍarīka-sūtra* and the Mahayana sutras expounded before and after the *Saddharmapuṇḍarīka-sūtra*. When the Buddha expounded the *Saddharmapuṇḍarīka-sūtra*, Śāriputra and other *śrāvaka*s, great bodhisattvas, gods, and men were so astonished at the differences that they thought that the *Saddharmapuṇḍarīka-sūtra* might have been expounded by "Māra in the form of the Buddha." The dim-eyed scholars of the Kegon, Hossō, Sanron, Shingon, and Nembutsu Sects do not notice these differences. They say that the sutras of their sects are not different from the *Saddharmapuṇḍarīka-sūtra* because their sutras are also Mahayana, just as the *Saddharmapuṇḍarīka-sūtra* is.

Some people in the lifetime of the Buddha may have believed in the *Saddharmapuṇḍarīka-sūtra* and abandoned the sutras expounded before the *Saddharmapuṇḍarīka-sūtra* during the first forty and odd years. But it is very difficult for the people who appeared after the extinction of the Buddha to believe in this sutra because (1) the earlier sutras have many themes, but this sutra has only one theme, (2) the earlier sutras are many in number, but this sutra is only one, and (3) the earlier sutras were expounded during so long a time as forty-odd years, but this sutra was expounded during only eight years.

Many people say, "The Buddha is a great liar. We cannot believe him. If we must believe in something, we shall probably believe in the earlier sutras. We can never believe in the *Saddharmapuṇḍarīka-sūtra*."

Some say that they believe in the *Saddharmapuṇḍarīka-sūtra*, but the *Saddharmapuṇḍarīka-sūtra* they claim to believe in is not the *Saddharmapuṇḍarīka-sūtra* in its proper sense, because these people gladly follow the priests who say that the

Saddharmapuṇḍarīka-sūtra is not different from the *Mahāvairocana-sūtra, Avataṁsaka-sūtra,* or *Sukhāvatīvyūha-sūtra.* They do not follow the priests who say that the *Saddharmapuṇḍarīka-sūtra* is different from the other sutras. Even when they follow the latter,
213b they do so only superficially, not from the bottom of their hearts.

No one agrees with me when I say, "Since Buddhism was introduced into Japan more than seven hundred years ago, no one in Japan has read the *Saddharmapuṇḍarīka-sūtra* correctly except Dengyō Daishi." But what I say is consistent with the statement in the *Saddharmapuṇḍarīka-sūtra:*

> It is not difficult to grasp Mount Sumeru and hurl it to a distance of countless Buddha worlds.... It is difficult to expound this sutra in the evil world after the extinction of the Buddha.

According to the *Mahāparinirvāṇa-sūtra,* which was expounded as a supplement to the *Saddharmapuṇḍarīka-sūtra,* the slanderers of the right teachings of the Buddha in the defiled world of the Age of Degeneration are more numerous than the keepers of the right teachings of the Buddha, just as the particles of earth of the worlds of the ten quarters are more numerous than the particles of earth put on a nail. What do you think of this? Are the people of Japan the particles of earth on a nail? Am I the particles of earth of the worlds of the ten quarters? Think it over! Justice will win in the reign of a wise king. But justice will have to yield to injustice in the reign of a stupid monarch. You should know that the true significance of the *Saddharmapuṇḍarīka-sūtra* will be revealed in the world of a saint.

It seems that the sutras expounded before the *Saddharmapuṇḍarīka-sūtra* are more attractive than the first fourteen chapters of the *Saddharmapuṇḍarīka-sūtra.* But if the earlier sutras are more attractive [and more valuable], Śāriputra and other adherents of the two vehicles would have lost a chance to become Buddhas forever. How sad it would be for them!

The Eternity of Śākyamuni Buddha

The other of the two [most important teachings of the *Saddharma-puṇḍarīka-sūtra* is that Śākyamuni Buddha is eternal].

Our Lord Teacher Śākyamuni, the World-honored One, was born in the latter half of the ninth *antara* kalpa of the kalpa of maintenance, when the average age of men had been reduced to a hundred years. He was a grandson of King Siṁhahunu, and the first son of King Śuddhodana. In his childhood, he was called Crown Prince Siddhārtha or All Teaching Accomplished Bodhisattva. He renounced his family at the age of nineteen, and attained enlightenment at the age of thirty. At the place of enlightenment, he was ceremonially rewarded with the lordship of the Lotus King world. He expounded the great wonderful teachings of the ten propositions, the six characteristics of all things, the perfect harmony of all things, and the sudden way of attaining enlightenment. All the Buddhas of the world of the ten quarters appeared, and all bodhisattvas assembled. Can it be that the Buddha kept the Great Dharma unexpounded in such circumstances, provided with the wonderful world and excellent hearers and also with the appearance of the Buddhas?

The Buddha said in the *Avataṁsaka-sūtra,* "I expound the perfect sutra with my power of freedom." The *Avataṁsaka-sūtra* is compiled in sixty volumes. Every letter of the sutra is perfect 213c
just as every *cintāmaṇi* gem is as brilliant as a chain of innumerable *cintāmaṇi* gems. A single gem is as brilliant as a chain of gems and a chain of gems is not more brilliant than a single gem. In the same manner, a letter of the *Avataṁsaka-sūtra* is as perfect as the whole sutra while the sutra is not more perfect than a letter. It says in this sutra, "Our mind is equal to the mind of the Buddha and also of all living beings." This teaching is the core not only of the Kegon Sect but also of the Hossō, Sanron, Shingon, and Tendai Sects. How can it be that the Buddha kept his teachings unrevealed in such a wonderful sutra?

The Buddha said in this sutra, however, that adherents of the two vehicles and the *icchantika*s cannot become Buddhas. This statement of the Buddha is like a flaw in a precious stone. He also said as many as three times in this sutra that he attained enlightenment for the first time during his life in this world. He never revealed in this sutra that he attained Buddhahood in the remotest past as he did in the "Chapter on the Duration of the Life of the Tathāgata" in the *Saddharmapuṇḍarīka-sūtra*. From this we must say that the *Avataṁsaka-sūtra* is like a broken gem, the moon covered with clouds, or the eclipsed sun. It is very strange.

What is lacking in the *Avataṁsaka-sūtra* cannot be found in the Āgama sutras, the Vaipulya sutras, the *Mahāprajñā-pāramitā-sūtra,* or the *Mahāvairocana-sūtra,* because these sutras are worthless when compared with the *Avataṁsaka-sūtra,* although they are honorable in so far as they are expounded by the Buddha. The Buddha says in the Āgama sutras, "I attained enlightenment for the first time." It says in the *Mahāsaṁnipāta-sūtra,* "It is sixteen years since the Tathāgata attained enlightenment." The *Vimalakīrtinirdésa-sūtra* reads, "The Buddha sat under the tree for the first time and defeated devils with his power." The Buddha says in the *Mahāvairocana-sūtra,* "I once sat at the place of enlightenment." In the *Ninnō-hannya-kyō* (*Jen-wang-pan-jo-ching*) the Buddha says, "It is twenty-nine years since I attained Buddhahood." It goes without saying that these sutras do not reveal the eternity of the Buddha.

But what astonishes us is that the Buddha says in the *Muryōgi-kyō* (*Wu-liang-i-ching*), "I was able to attain *anuttara-samyak-saṁbodhi* at the end of a period of six years of sitting under the bodhi tree at the place of enlightenment." The *Muryōgi-kyō* is wonderful because in this sutra the Buddha criticized great teachings such as the teaching of "all is mind" in the *Avataṁsaka-sūtra,* the teaching of the sea emblem *samādhi,* and the teaching of "enlightenment, illusions–not two," these last two teachings being expounded in the Vaipulya sutras and the *Mahāprajñāpāramitā-sūtra.* The Buddha said that these teachings were expounded before he declared, "I have not yet revealed my true teaching," and that these teachings would require the practice of many kalpas. Yet his statement of the historicity of his Buddhahood in this *Muryōgi-kyō* is consistent with his statement in the *Avataṁsaka-sūtra* that the Buddha attained enlightenment for the first time during his life in this world. How strange!

[We know that an introduction to a book sometimes omits mentioning some of the main points of the whole writing. Therefore,] maybe we can say that the *Muryōgi-kyō* does not refer to the eternity of the Buddha because it is an introduction to the 214a
Saddharmapuṇḍarīka-sūtra. But what perplexes us most is that [the first fourteen chapters of the *Saddharmapuṇḍarīka-sūtra* do not refer to the eternity of the Buddha].

The Buddha says in the section on the unification of the three vehicles into the One Vehicle in the principal part of the *Saddharmapuṇḍarīka-sūtra:*

> Only the Buddha attained the highest Truth, that is, the reality of all things.... As a rule, the World-honored One expounds the true teaching only after a long period of expounding expedient teachings.... I have laid aside all expedient teachings.

Prabhūtaratna Buddha supports the truthfulness of the eight chapters [from Chapter II to Chapter IX], which are included in the first fourteen chapters of the *Saddharmapuṇḍarīka-sūtra*. This gives us the impression that the Buddha did not conceal any of his teachings in the first fourteen chapters. But the reality is that the Buddha did not tell of the longevity of his life in these chapters. Instead, he says:

> I for the first time sat at the place of enlightenment and attained enlightenment. For three weeks after that, I gazed at the tree, or walked about.

This is most unthinkable.

In the "Chapter on Bodhisattvas from Underground" in the *Saddharmapuṇḍarīka-sūtra,* great bodhisattvas appear who have never been seen in this Sahā world for the past forty and more years. The Buddha says, "I taught them, and caused them to aspire to enlightenment."

Maitreya Bodhisattva asks the Buddha, saying:

> When you, the Tathāgata, were Crown Prince [Siddhārtha], you left the palace of the Śākyas, sat at the place of enlightenment not far from the city of Gayā, and attained *anuttara-samyak-saṁbodhi.* It is only forty or so years since then. World-honored One! How did you do these great deeds of the Buddha in such a short time?

In order to clear up his doubts, the Lord Teacher Śākyamuni, the World-honored One, refers to the hearers of the earlier sutras and also to the first fourteen chapters of the *Saddharmapuṇḍarīka-sūtra,* saying at the beginning of the "Chapter on the Duration of the Life of the Tathāgata" in the *Saddharmapuṇḍarīka-sūtra:*

> The gods, men, and *asura*s in the world think that I, Śākyamuni Buddha, left the palace of the Śākyas, sat at the place of enlightenment not far from the city of Gayā, and attained *anuttara-samyak-saṁbodhi* [forty and odd years ago].

Then he clears up Maitreya's doubts, saying, "To tell the truth, good men, it is many hundreds of thousands of billions of nayutas of kalpas since I became the Buddha."

The *Avataṁsaka-sūtra, Mahāprajñāpāramitā-sūtra,* and *Mahāvairocana-sūtra* conceal not only the possibility of attaining Buddhahood by adherents of the two vehicles but also Śākyamuni Buddha's attainment of Buddhahood in the remotest past. These sutras have two faults. First, they still preserve the differences between the three vehicles; therefore, their teachings are merely expedient. They do not reveal the teaching of one mind–three thousand expounded in the first fourteen chapters of the *Saddharmapuṇḍarīka-sūtra*. Second, they hold that Śākyamuni Buddha attained Buddhahood during his life in this world. Therefore, Śākyamuni Buddha attained Buddhahood during his life in this world. Therefore, the Śākyamuni Buddha in these sutras is historical, not original. The Original Buddha reveals his originality in the "Discourse of the Original Buddha," which covers the second fourteen chapters of the *Saddharmapuṇḍarīka-sūtra*. These two great teachings are the essence of all the teachings of the Buddha, and the core of all the sutras.

In the "Chapter on Expedients," which is included in the "Discourse of the Historical Buddha," the Buddha expounds the teaching of one mind–three thousand, and accordingly, the teaching of the possibility of attaining Buddhahood by adherents of the two vehicles, and thereby remedies the first fault of the earlier sutras. But the originality of the Buddha is not yet revealed there. Without the revelation of the originality of the Buddha, the teaching of one mind–three thousand is not perfect, and the possibility of attaining Buddhahood by adherents of the two vehicles is not se- 214b
cure. The teaching of one mind–three thousand expounded in the "Discourse of the Historical Buddha" is as fictitious as the moon reflected in the water or as rootless as a plant floating on a wave.

The historicity of Śākyamuni Buddha is disproved in the "Discourse of the Original Buddha." Accordingly, the differences between the four results to be achieved by the four kinds of teachings—Hinayana teachings, Mahayana-cum-Hinayana teachings, Specialized Mahayana teachings, and Perfect Mahayana teachings—are eliminated. The differences between the four causes of the four results are also eliminated. In the "Discourse of the Original Buddha," the beginninglessness of the causality of birth and death of living beings of the ten regions is established, and the causality of birth and death of living beings of the ten regions expounded in the earlier sutras and also in the first fourteen chapters of the *Saddharmapuṇḍarīka-sūtra* is eliminated. This is the teaching of causality revealed in the "Discourse of the Original Buddha." By this teaching, the nine regions other than the Buddha world exist in the beginningless Buddha world, and the Buddha world exists in every one of the nine other regions, which also have no beginning. Here we actually see that the ten regions involve each other, that the one hundred regions thus established each have ten suchnesses, making one thousand suchnesses. This eventually makes the teaching of one mind–three thousand expounded in the "Discourse of the Original Buddha."

Now we can say this. The scholars of the various sects are ignorant not only of what Buddha or Buddhas they are worshiping but also of the Buddha revealed in the "Chapter on the Duration of the Life of the Tathāgata" in the *Saddharmapuṇḍarīka-sūtra*. They do not know that the Buddhas on the lotus flowers revealed in the *Avataṁsaka-sūtra,* the Buddhas of the ten quarters, the small Śākyamuni Buddha as described in the Āgama sutras, and the Buddhas of the Provisional Mahayana revealed in the Vaipulya sutras, the *Mahāprajñāpāramitā-sūtra,* the *Suvarṇaprabhāsa-sūtra,* and the *Mahāvairocana-sūtra* are all manifestations of the Buddha revealed in the "Chapter on the Duration of the Life of the Tathāgata," just as the water contained in utensils of various sizes reflects the moon variously. They think that a reflection of the moon is the real moon, and try to grasp it or tie it with a rope. T'ien-t'ai says, "They do not know the real moon. They see only a reflection of the moon in the pond."

Even the assurance of Buddhahood for adherents of the two vehicles does not seem to be so attractive as the teachings expounded in the sutras before the *Saddharmapuṇḍarīka-sūtra*. The teaching that the Buddha attained enlightenment in the remotest past is incomparably less attractive than the teachings of the earlier sutras. The earlier sutras are more attractive than the *Saddharmapuṇḍarīka-sūtra,* and the "Discourse of the Historical Buddha," which covers the first fourteen chapters of the *Saddharmapuṇḍarīka-sūtra,* is more attractive than the second fourteen chapters of the sutra. Furthermore, although [the first two of the second fourteen chapters, that is,] the "Chapter on Bodhisattvas from Underground" and the "Chapter on the Duration of the Life of the Tathāgata" reveal the eternity of the Buddha, the rest of the second fourteen chapters recover the historicity of the Buddha.

The beginninglessness and endlessness of the *dharmakāya* of the Buddha is expounded in the *Mahāparinirvāṇa-sūtra* compiled in forty volumes, which was expounded by the Buddha on his deathbed between the two trees, and also in other Mahayana sutras expounded before the *Saddharmapuṇḍarīka-sūtra*. But the eternity of the *sambhogakāya* and *nirmāṇakāya* of the Buddha is not expounded in those sutras. The eternity of the *trikāya* of the Buddha is expounded only in the two chapters of the *Saddharmapuṇḍarīka-sūtra*. It is very difficult to persuade others to pick up only the two chapters of the *Saddharmapuṇḍarīka-sūtra*, that 214c
is, the "Chapter on Bodhisattvas from Underground" and the "Chapter on the Duration of the Life of the Tathāgata," and abandon all the other chapters of the sutra and also the vast amount of all the other sutras including the *Mahāparinirvāṇa-sūtra*.

The Hossō Sect was founded by Asaṅga Bodhisattva. There lived a great scholar called Asaṅga Bodhisattva in India, nine hundred years after the extinction of the Buddha. At night he ascended to the inner palace of the Tuṣita Heaven and studied the sacred teachings of the Buddha under the guidance of Maitreya Bodhisattva. In the daytime he propagated the teachings of the Hossō Sect in the country of Ayodhya. His disciples were Vasubandhu, Dharmapāla, Nanda, and Śīlabhadra. They were all great scholars. King Śīlāditya the Great bowed to Asaṅga Bodhisattva. The brahmans in the five districts of India leveled their banners before him and followed him. Hsüan-tsang San-tsang of China went to India, and stayed there for seventeen years. He visited more than a hundred and thirty countries in India. He followed the Hossō Sect, abandoning all the other sects. He introduced the Hossō Sect into China, and taught the teachings of that sect to Emperor T'ai-tsung (Taisō). Shen-fang (Shimbō), Chia-shang (Kashō), P'u-kuang (Fukō), and K'uei-chi (Kiki) became his disciples. He propagated the sect to more than three hundred sixty countries in China, having Ta-tz'u-en-ssu (Daijionji) as the headquarters of the sect. The sect was introduced into Japan by Dōji and Dōshō in the reign of the forty-fifth Emperor Shōmu. The headquarters of the sect were installed at Yamashina-dera Temple. This sect is probably the most prosperous sect in the three countries: India, China, and Japan.

The scholars of the sect criticize me, saying:

> In all the sutras, from the *Avataṁsaka-sūtra* expounded at the beginning of the teaching of the Buddha to the *Saddharmapuṇḍarīka-sūtra* and the *Mahāparinirvāṇa-sūtra* expounded at the end of his teaching, the Buddha says that those who do not have the Buddha-nature and those who adhere to the two vehicles can never become Buddhas. The Buddha is not double-tongued. His statement that they can never become Buddhas is unchangeable even if the sun and the moon fall to the ground or even if the earth is turned upside down. In the *Saddharmapuṇḍarīka-sūtra* or the *Mahāparinirvāṇa-sūtra,* the Buddha never says that those who do not have the Buddha-nature and those who adhere to the two vehicles, both of whom are criticized in the earlier sutras, will become Buddhas by mentioning their names. Close your eyes and think it over! If the *Saddharmapuṇḍarīka-sūtra* or the *Mahāparinirvāṇa-sūtra* contains the Buddha's statement that adherents of the two vehicles and people without the Buddha-nature can become Buddhas,
> 215a can it be that great scholars such as Asaṅga and Vasubandhu and Tripiṭaka teachers such as Hsüan-tsang and Tz'u-en overlooked that statement, made no comment on it, did not credit it, and made no efforts to propagate it? Did Asaṅga not ask Maitreya about that statement? You say that you follow the words of the *Saddharmapuṇḍarīka-sūtra.* But you believe only the prejudiced views of T'ien-t'ai, Miao-le, and Dengyō, and you read the sutra with their prejudices. Therefore, you say that the *Saddharmapuṇḍarīka-sūtra* is as different from the earlier sutras as water is from fire.

The Kegon and Shingon Sects are far more excellent than the Hossō and Sanron Sects. They criticize me, saying:

It is clear that the assurance of Buddhahood for adherents of the two vehicles and the eternity of Śākyamuni Buddha are expounded not only in the *Saddharmapuṇḍarīka-sūtra* but also in the *Avataṁsaka-sūtra* and the *Mahāvairocana-sūtra*. Tu-shun (Tojun), Chih-yen (Chigon), Fa-tsang (Hōzō), and Ch'eng-kuan (Chōkan) of the Kegon Sect, and Śubhākarasiṁha, Vajrabodhi, and Amoghavajra of the Shingon Sect are far more respectable than T'ien-t'ai and Dengyō. Śubhākarasiṁha and others were the orthodox successors of the Dharma from Mahāvairocana Tathāgata. There is no doubt that these successors never committed mistakes because they were reincarnations of the Buddha. It says in the *Avataṁsaka-sūtra* that it is an inconceivable number of kalpas since Śākyamuni attained Buddhahood. The Buddha says in the *Mahāvairocana-sūtra* that he is the origin of all. How can you say that the eternity of Śākyamuni Buddha is expounded only in the "Chapter on the Duration of the Life of the Tathāgata" in the *Saddharmapuṇḍarīka-sūtra*? A frog in a well does not know the ocean. You are like the frog or like a woodsman who does not know the capital city. Do you read only the "Chapter on the Duration of the Life of the Tathāgata"? Do you not know the *Avataṁsaka-sūtra* and the *Mahāvairocana-sūtra*? I ask you more. Do the scholars of India, China, Silla, and Pekche also say that the assurance of Buddhahood of the adherents to the two vehicles and the eternity of Śākyamuni Buddha are expounded only in the *Saddharmapuṇḍarīka-sūtra*?

It is true that the sutra expounded during the last eight years of the Buddha's teaching is different from the sutras expounded during the forty and odd years before that. It is also true that, when a latter statement contradicts a former statement, we should follow the latter statement. Notwithstanding this, however, the earlier sutras are more attractive than the *Saddharmapuṇḍarīka-sūtra*.

The *Saddharmapuṇḍarīka-sūtra* may have been duly appreciated in the lifetime of the Buddha, but most of the scholars who appeared after the extinction of the Buddha have favored the earlier sutras. It was difficult to believe the *Saddharmapuṇḍarīka-sūtra* even when it was first expounded. It is more difficult in this
215b Age of Degeneration, when saints and sages are decreasing in number, and when perverted people are increasing instead. Today, even secular matters are apt to be mishandled. Needless to say, profound teachings of the spiritual world are liable to be misunderstood. Even the clever teachers of the Vātsīputrīya and Vaipulya Sects did not know the difference between Mahayana and Hinayana. Even wise men such as [a person known in China as] Wu-kou (Muku) and [a person whose name is transliterated as] Mo-t'a (Matō) could not distinguish true teachings from provisional teachings. These sects were founded in India in the Age of the Right Teachings of the Buddha, that is, during the one thousand years after the extinction of the Buddha. From this we can say that the teachings of the Buddha were misunderstood even in their birthplace not so long after the extinction of the Buddha. People who were born long after the extinction of the Buddha in remote countries such as China and Japan, where languages are different, are less clever, die younger, and have more greed, more anger, and more stupidity. There is no wonder that none of them understands the Buddhist sutras correctly.

The Buddha says in the *Mahāparinirvāṇa-sūtra:*

> In the Age of Degeneration, the keepers of the right teachings of the Buddha will be fewer than the slanderers of his teachings, just as the particles of earth put on a nail are fewer than those of earth composing the worlds of the ten quarters.

He also says in the *Hōmetsujin-kyō* (*Fa-mieh-chin-ching*):

> The keepers of the right teachings of the Buddha will be fewer than the slanderers of his teachings, just as a pebble or two are fewer than the particles of sands in the Ganges River.

There will be hardly one person who keeps the right teachings of the Buddha in the five hundred or one thousand years to come. [Many] people will be sent to the evil regions due to committing worldly crimes. But they are much fewer than those who are sent to the evil regions for slandering the Dharma of the Buddha, just as the particles of earth put on a nail are fewer than the particles of earth composing the worlds of the ten quarters. More priests will be sent there than laymen; more nuns than laywomen.

Chapter II

Am I Not the Practitioner of the *Saddharmapuṇḍarīka-sūtra*?

Why Am I Persecuted?

Now I reflect on myself. I was born poor and mean in a remote country more than two hundred years after the beginning of the Age of Degeneration. When I was transmigrating from one to another of the six regions in my previous existences, I might have been a great king, who ruled the people just as a high wind sways the twigs of small trees, but I could not become a Buddha; or I might have been a bodhisattva who performed the bodhisattva practices through all the stages of practice, starting with the lowest stage of under-saintship, then the higher stage of under-saintship for a kalpa, two kalpas, and up to innumerable kalpas according to the regulations stipulated in the Mahayana and Hinayana sutras, and approached the final stage of irrevocability, but I could not become a Buddha, hindered by obstinate obstacles. Or was I excluded from the third kind of living beings whom Mahābhijñājñānābhibhū Tathāgata assured of their attainment of Buddhahood in or after the lifetime of Śākyamuni Buddha? Or does my indolence bar me from becoming a Buddha even though I was given the seed of Buddhahood by Śākyamuni Buddha five hundred thousand billion *nayuta asaṁkhya* kalpas ago? Because 215c
I am practicing the *Saddharmapuṇḍarīka-sūtra*, evil people, the government, heretics, and adherents of the Hinayana sutras have persecuted me. I have endured all this.

Those who followed Tao-ch'o (Dōshaku), Shan-tao (Zendō), and Hōnen are now in the evil regions. Tao-ch'o, Shan-tao, and Hōnen seem to have thoroughly studied both the True Mahayana sutras and the Provisional Mahayana sutras, but they were possessed by devils. They enhanced the *Saddharmapuṇḍarīka-sūtra* but deprecated people, saying:

> The *Saddharmapuṇḍarīka-sūtra* is too profound for people to understand.... No one has yet attained Buddhahood by means of the *Saddharmapuṇḍarīka-sūtra*. Not one among one thousand people.

People had been told so innumerable times throughout their innumerable previous existences. Therefore, they followed those priests and believed the Provisional Mahayana sutras. In the course of time, they backslid from the Provisional Mahayana sutras to the Hinayana sutras, then to Brahmanism and Confucianism. At last they fell into the evil regions.

I know this. In Japan, only I know this. But if I say this, my parents, brothers, and masters will be persecuted by the government. If I do not say this, it seems that I have no compassion toward others. What shall I do?

In order to decide, I consulted the *Saddharmapuṇḍarīka-sūtra* and the *Mahāparinirvāṇa-sūtra,* and found that if I do not say this, I may be peaceful in my present life but I shall fall into the Hell of Incessant Suffering in my next life, and that if I do, I shall definitely have to suffer the three obstacles and meet the four devils. My decision was, "I must say this, I must not keep silent. It is better not to start saying this than to stop saying this halfway for fear that I shall be persecuted by the government and others."

When I was thinking this, I was reminded of the six difficulties and the nine easinesses expounded in the "Chapter on Beholding the Stupa of Treasures" in the *Saddharmapuṇḍarīka-sūtra*. According to this chapter, we may be able to hurl Mount Sumeru even though we are weak. We may be able to shoulder a load of hay and stay unburned in the fire at the end of the kalpa of destruction even though we have no supernatural powers. We may be able to read and memorize as many sutras as there are sands in the Ganges River even though we have no wisdom. But it is very difficult for us to keep even a phrase or a *gāthā* of the *Saddharmapuṇḍarīka-sūtra* during this Age of Degeneration. I believe that all this is meant by the chapter. From my determined aspiration for enlightenment, I have made a vow never to retreat from the propagation of the *Saddharmapuṇḍarīka-sūtra.*

For the past twenty-odd years, I have been propagating the teachings of the *Saddharmapuṇḍarīka-sūtra.* Persecutions have ensued day after day, month after month, year after year. Small troubles were numerous. Big ones were four. Two of them I do not relate here. The other two were caused by the government. This 216a
time it was almost fatal to me. Furthermore, my disciples and lay followers, and also the people who happened to come to hear me, were severely punished like traitors.

The Buddha says in Volume IV of the *Saddharmapuṇḍarīka-sūtra,* "Many people hate this sutra with jealousy even in my lifetime. Needless to say, more people will do so after my extinction." He says in Volume II of the sutra:

> Some will despise the person who reads, recites, copies, or keeps this sutra. They will hate him, look at him with jealousy, and harbor enmity against him.

He says in Volume VI of the sutra:

> I did not expound this sutra before because, if I had done so, many people in the world would have hated this sutra and few would have believed it.

The bodhisattvas say in the same volume of the sutra:

> Ignorant people will speak ill of us, and abuse us.... They will say to kings, ministers, brahmans, and householders, "They have wrong views. They are expounding the teachings of heretics...." They will drive us out of our monasteries from time to time.

It says in Volume VII of the sutra, "The people struck Never Despising Bodhisattva with a stick, a piece of wood, a piece of tile, and a stone."

It says in the *Mahāparinirvāṇa-sūtra:*

> Thereupon many brahmans came together to King Ajātaśatru of Magadha, and said, "Here is a very evil man. His name is Gautama Śramaṇa. All the evil men in the world went to him and followed him only for gain. They do not do any good. They subjugated Kāśyapa, Śāriputra, Maudgalyāyana, and others by their supernatural powers."

T'ien-t'ai says, "Needless to say, more people will hate this sutra after the extinction of the Buddha. It will be more difficult to save them."

Miao-le says:

> Hatred against the keeper of the right teachings of the Buddha is held by those who have not yet eliminated illusions. Jealousy of him is roused by those who are not joyful of hearing him.

T'ien-t'ai was treated as an enemy by the leaders of the three sects in South China and the seven sects in North China, and also by all the other scholars of China.

Tokuichi says:

> Poor Chih-i! Whose disciple are you? With your tongue shorter than three inches, you slander the Dharma expounded by the Buddha with his broad and long tongue.

Chih-tu (Chido) of Tung-ch'in (Tōjun) says:

> Question: Many people hated this sutra with jealousy even in the lifetime of the Buddha. Those who propagate this sutra after the extinction of the Buddha will have to face many difficulties. Why?
>
> Answer: The proverb says that a good medicine tastes bitter. This sutra eliminates the differences between the five

kinds of living beings, and establishes the teaching of the One Vehicle. Therefore, this sutra criticizes not only laymen but also priests [who think that they are different from laymen]. It rejects not only the Hinayana but also the Mahayana [which is regarded as entirely different from the Hinayana]. It calls gods and *māras* "vermin" and brahmans "devils." It says that adherents of the Hinayana are base and mean and that the bodhisattvas are just beginners in the Way of the Buddha. Therefore, gods and *māras* hate to listen to this sutra. Brahmans cover their ears, adherents of the two vehicles are frightened, and bodhisattvas become timid. All these people persecute the propagator of this sutra. This sutra's statement that more people will hate this sutra with jealousy after the extinction of the Buddha is quite true.

Dengyō says in his *Kenkairon:*

The representatives of the priests of the six Nara Sects said to the emperor, "There was once a sophisticated brahman in India. Now here is a quibbling baldheaded man. Possessed 216b
by devils, he deceives people."

I said to the emperor, "Once in the Period of Ch'i (Sei), Kuang-t'ung (Kōtō) attempted to kill Bodhidharma. Now the priests of the six Nara sects speak ill of me." The Buddha was right in saying, "Needless to say, more people will hate this sutra with jealousy after my extinction."

Dengyō also says in his *Hokke-shūku:*

I am living toward the end of the Age of the Counterfeit of the Right Teachings of the Buddha. The Age of Degeneration is coming. The country where I live is east of T'ang (Tō) and west of Chieh (Katsu). The people of this country have five defilements. It is the Age of Conflicts. The Buddha was right in saying, "Many people hate this sutra with jealousy even in my lifetime. Needless to say, more people will do so after my extinction."

Father and mother will be hated by their child when they cauterize its skin with moxa to cure its disease. A man who is seriously ill is not willing to take good but bitter medicine. Many people hated this sutra with jealousy even in the lifetime of the Buddha. More people did so in the Age of the Counterfeit of the Right Teachings of the Buddha. Many more people will do so in this Age of Degeneration in a country far from India. There will be mountain after mountain, billow after billow, difficulty after difficulty, injustice after injustice in my way.

In the middle of the Age of the Counterfeit of the Right Teachings of the Buddha, only T'ien-t'ai read the *Saddharmapuṇḍarīka-sūtra* and all the other sutras correctly. The leaders of the three sects in South China and the seven sects in North China criticized him, but were silenced during the debates that took place before the emperors of the Ch'en and Sui dynasties. Toward the end of the Age of the Counterfeit of the Right Teachings of the Buddha, only Dengyō read the *Saddharmapuṇḍarīka-sūtra* and all the other sutras correctly. The priests of the seven great temples of Nara criticized him, but were silenced when Emperors Kammu, Heizei, and Saga decided that Dengyō was right.

Now more than two hundred years have already elapsed since the beginning of the Age of Degeneration. Because the Buddha said, "Needless to say . . . after my extinction" and because it is already the Age of Conflicts, injustice is preferred in order to mark the defilement of the world. I was not permitted to have a public debate, but was exiled and was about to be killed.

I am far from T'ien-t'ai and Dengyō in understanding the *Saddharmapuṇḍarīka-sūtra,* but they would be astonished to find that I am far more patient of hardships and far more compassionate toward others than they.

Why Do the Gods Not Protect Me?

I expected that the gods would protect me, but they have not yet done so. My hardships are increasing all the more. I want to learn from all this. Am I not the practitioner of the *Saddharma-puṇḍarīka-sūtra*? Have the gods left this country? I am very doubtful of this. 216c

If I had not been born in this country, the verses in the "Chapter on Encouragement of Keeping the Sutra" in Volume V of the *Saddharmapuṇḍarīka-sūtra* would have turned into dead letters, the Buddha who expounded this sutra would have become a great liar, and the eighty billion *nayuta*s of bodhisattvas who sang these verses would have been charged with falsehood like Devadatta. For the verses read, "Ignorant people will speak ill of us, abuse us, and threaten us with swords, sticks, tiles, or stones." Who else was spoken ill of, abused, and threatened with swords or sticks for the cause of the *Saddharmapuṇḍarīka-sūtra* in this age than I? Without me, the prophecy of this verse would become a lie.

The verses also run:

> Some *bhikṣus* in the evil world will be cunning. They will be ready to flatter others.... They will expound the Dharma to men of white robes. They will be respected by the people of the world as arhats who have the six supernatural powers.

This means that without the priests of the Nembutsu, Zen, and Ritsu Sects of today, the World-honored One would become a great liar.

It says in the verses, "In order to... slander us in the midst of the great multitude... they will say to kings, ministers, brahmans, and householders...." Unless the priests of today slandered me before the government and had me exiled, these verses would become dead letters.

It also says in the verses, "They will... drive us out of our monasteries from time to time." Unless I had been exiled more than once, where would be the truthfulness of the statement "from time to time"? Even T'ien-t'ai or Dengyō did not "read by body" [experience] the statement "from time to time." Needless to say, no one else did so. Only I did so because I am living at the beginning of the Age of Degeneration in the dreadful evil world that the Buddha predicted.

All the Buddha's prophecies have turned out true so far. The Buddha said in the *Fuhōzō-kyō* (*Fu-fa-ts'ang-ching*), "A great king named Aśoka will appear one hundred years after my extinction." He said in the *Mahāmāyā-sūtra,* "A man named Nāgārjuna Bodhisattva will appear in South India six hundred years after my extinction." He also said in the *Mahākaruṇā-sūtra,* "A man named Madhyāntika will transform the sea that covers the palace of dragons into land sixty years after my extinction." All these prophecies turned out true. If not, who would believe the teachings of the Buddha?

The Buddha said that the practitioner of the *Saddharmapuṇḍarīka-sūtra* will face enemies "in the dreadful evil world," in "the Age of Degeneration when the Dharma is about to be destroyed," or in "the last five hundred years." This determination of the time is invariably given in both of the Chinese versions of
217a the *Saddharmapuṇḍarīka-sūtra:* the *Myōhōrenge-kyō* (*Miao-fa-lien-hua-ching*) and the *Shōhoke-kyō* (*Cheng-fa-hua-ching*). Who will believe and receive the words of the Buddha if we have not the three kinds of enemies of the *Saddharmapuṇḍarīka-sūtra* today? Who is the practitioner of the *Saddharmapuṇḍarīka-sūtra* to prove the truthfulness of the words of the Buddha except me? The priests of the three sects in South China and the seven sects in North China and the priests of the seven great temples of Nara were enemies of the *Saddharmapuṇḍarīka-sūtra* in the Age of the Counterfeit of the Right Teachings of the Buddha. Needless to say, the priests of the Zen, Ritsu, and Nembutsu Sects of today cannot be excluded from these enemies. What I have done is consistent with the prophecy of the Buddha given in the sutra. I shall be happier if I am persecuted more.

A Hinayana bodhisattva, who had not yet eliminated all illusions, "did evil karmas by his own will." He saw his parents suffering severely in hell. Wishing to save them, he did evil karmas by his own will, went to hell, and gladly suffered together with his parents. I am like him. My suffering at present is unbearable, but I am glad to say that due to my present sufferings I shall be able to emancipate myself from the evil regions in my future life.

The only thing that the people of the world doubt, and I also doubt, is: Why do the gods not help me? The gods vowed to protect the practitioner of the *Saddharmapuṇḍarīka-sūtra*. They should immediately come and protect anyone who calls himself a practitioner of the *Saddharmapuṇḍarīka-sūtra* in order to fulfill their vow, even if that self-appointed practitioner of the *Saddharmapuṇḍarīka-sūtra* is as foolish as a monkey. They do not. Am I not the practitioner of the *Saddharmapuṇḍarīka-sūtra*? This question is the core of this writing and the most important thing of my life. Therefore, I will deal with this question from various angles in order to emphasize its importance, and then determine the correct answer to this question.

Chi-cha (Kisatsu) left home on official business. On the way to his destination, he was warmly treated by the lord of the country of Hsü (Jo). The lord wished to have the sword of Chi-cha, but did not express his wish. Chi-cha read the mind of the lord, and decided to give it to him on his way home to repay his hospitality. When he revisited Hsü, the lord was already dead. Chi-cha visited the tomb of the lord and offered his sword to the tombstone. Wang-yin (Ō-in) drank the water of a river, and put a coin into the river as a token of his gratitude to the river. Kung-yin, who failed to save his lord, killed himself by cutting open his abdomen, pulling the liver from his lord's body, and thrusting it into his own body. All these people were wise men. I think that they did so in order to repay the favors given by others. 217b

Why Do the *Śrāvaka*s Not Protect Me?

Needless to say, Śāriputra, Kāśyapa, and other *śrāvaka*s observed the two hundred fifty precepts and the three thousand deportments without fail. They eliminated illusions caused by false judgment and evil desire. They were great saints. They released themselves from the triple world. They were the teachers of Brahma, Śakra, and other gods, and the eyes of all living beings.

Although they were condemned as persons disqualified from ever becoming Buddhas in the sutras expounded during the first forty and more years, they were given the elixir of life made from the *Saddharmapuṇḍarīka-sūtra* and are now allowed to become Buddhas, just as a parched seed brings forth a bud, as a broken stone recovers its original form, or as a dead tree bears flowers and fruit. Although they have not yet completed the procedure to attain Buddhahood through eight stages, they should repay the great favors given by this sutra. If they do not, they will be nothing but animals because animals do not know the favors given by others. If they do not, those *śrāvaka*s will be inferior to the Chinese sages mentioned previously. Mao-pao (Mō-hō) traded a fisherman his robe for a turtle and released the turtle into the sea. Mao-pao was defeated in battle, and he plunged into the sea. The turtle that had been saved by him came and rescued him. The turtle had not forgotten his favor. A big fish in the pond of K'un-ming (Kommei) was released by Emperor Wu-ti of the Han dynasty. The fish presented him with a brilliant gem at night. Even those animals repayed the favors given by others. Needless to say, the great saints should do so.

Venerable Ānanda was the second son of King Droṇodana. Venerable Rāhula was a grandson of King Śuddhodana. They were born of royal families and attained arhatship. But they were prohibited from becoming Buddhas before the *Saddharma-puṇḍarīka-sūtra* was expounded. In the *Saddharmapuṇḍarīka-sūtra,* they were for the first time given the names of Tathāgatas, Sāgaravaradharabuddhivikrīḍitābhijña and Saptaratna-padmavikrāntagāmin, respectively, during the session on Mount Sacred Eagle. The session was held during the last eight years of the teaching of the Buddha. Without the *Saddharmapuṇḍarīka-sūtra,* no one will respect a person deprived of Buddhahood even though he is a noble and great saint. [A *śrāvaka* without Buddhahood is like a king without virtue.] A king deserves the name insofar as he can be relied on by the people. King Chieh (Ketsu) of the Hsia (Ka) dynasty and King Chou of the Yin dynasty misruled the people and destroyed their own countries. Therefore, even today evil persons are called "Chieh-Chou." Even an ignoble man or a leper will get angry when he is called "Chieh-Chou," thinking that he is spoken ill of.

The twelve hundred *śrāvaka*s were for the first time assured of their Buddhahood in the *Saddharmapuṇḍarīka-sūtra*. So were 217c the other innumerable *śrāvaka*s. Without the *Saddharma-puṇḍarīka-sūtra,* no one would be glad to hear the names of these *śrāvaka*s who were deprived of Buddhahood. One thousand *śrāvaka*s compiled the Tripiṭaka. No one would read the Tripiṭaka compiled by people without Buddhahood. No one would make their pictures or images for worship.

I think that arhats are worshiped only because they were assured of Buddhahood in the *Saddharmapuṇḍarīka-sūtra*. Without the *Saddharmapuṇḍarīka-sūtra, śrāvaka*s would be as powerless as a fish taken out of water, as a monkey without trees, as a babe without milk, or as a subject without a king. Therefore, they should protect the practitioner of the *Saddharmapuṇḍarīka-sūtra*.

The *śrāvaka*s obtained heavenly eyes and the eyes of wisdom, in addition to their natural eyes, by hearing the sutras expounded before the *Saddharmapuṇḍarīka-sūtra,* and the eyes of the Dharma and the eyes of the Buddha by hearing the *Saddharma-puṇḍarīka-sūtra*. They can see the worlds of the ten quarters. Needless to say, they can see the practitioner of the *Saddharma-puṇḍarīka-sūtra* in this Sahā world. Even if I am an evil man, and abuse the *śrāvaka*s, threaten them with a sword or a stick, or speak ill of them, not in merely a word or two but in many words for a year or two, for a kalpa or two kalpas or a hundred thousand billion kalpas, they should not desert me insofar as I am the practitioner of the *Saddharmapuṇḍarīka-sūtra*. Father and mother will not abandon their child even when it abuses them. A mother owl brings up her owlet although she knows that it will eat her when it grows up. A father *hakyō,* a wild animal, takes care of his young although he knows that it will kill him when it becomes an adult. Even animals love and protect their offspring although their offspring are their future enemies. Needless to say, it cannot be that great saints like the *śrāvaka*s desert the practitioner of the *Saddharmapuṇḍarīka-sūtra*.

When the four great *śrāvaka*s understood the Dharma, they addressed the Buddha:

> We are *śrāvaka*s in the true sense of the word. We will cause all living beings to hear the voice telling of the enlightenment of the Buddha. We are arhats in the true sense of the word. All gods, men, *māra*s, and Brahmas in the worlds should make offerings to us. You, the World-honored One, are the great benefactor. By doing this rare thing, you taught and benefited us out of your compassion toward us. No one will be able to repay your favors even if he tries to do so for many hundreds of millions of kalpas. No one will be able to repay your favors even if he bows to you respectfully and offers you his hands, feet, or anything else. No one will be able to repay your favors even if he carries you on his head or shoulders and respects you from the bottom of his heart for as many kalpas as there are sands in the
> 218a Ganges River, or even if he offers you delicious food, innumerable treasured garments, much bedding, and various medicines, or even if he erects a stupa-mausoleum made of the cow-head *candana* and adorns it with treasures, or even if he covers the ground with treasured garments and offers them to the Buddha for as many kalpas as there are sands in the Ganges River.

The *śrāvaka*s were criticized in the earlier sutras. These sutras can be compared to the first four of the five tastes. The *śrāvaka*s were blamed in the presence of a great multitude of gods and men innumerable times. The cry of Venerable Kāśyapa reverberated over one thousand million Sumeru worlds. The stunned Venerable Subhūti dropped his alms bowl. Śāriputra vomited all he had eaten [when he heard that he did not deserve offerings]. Pūrṇa was contemptuously likened to feces in a beautiful vase.

In the Āgama sutras expounded by the Buddha at the Deer Park, the World-honored One enthusiastically praised the *śrāvaka*s for observing the two hundred fifty precepts, and told the multitude to respect them as their teachers. But now he denied what he had expounded in the Āgama sutras. This is apparently contradictory.

The World-honored One also contradicted himself in another case. He abused Devadatta, saying, "You are a fool. You eat the spit of someone else." Hearing this, Devadatta felt as if he had been shot in the chest with a poisonous arrow. He reproached the Buddha, saying to others:

> Gautama is not the Buddha. I am the eldest son of King Droṇodana, the eldest brother of Venerable Ānanda, and a member of the Gautama family. He should advise me personally if I am wrong. Now he says such a bad thing before this great multitude of gods and men. Can we call him the Great Man or the Buddha? He was once the enemy of my wife. Now he is the enemy of this congregation. From now I will be his great enemy.

Some of the great *śrāvaka*s were born into the families of brahmans or rich men. Therefore, they were patronized by kings and respected by laymen. Some of them were born into noble families or were rich themselves. But once they followed the Buddha, they abandoned worldly fame, leveled the banner of arrogance, 218b
took off lay garments, wore robes of cast-off rags, threw away insect-sweepers of white hair and bows and arrows, and carried alms bowls like poor men or beggars. They had no houses to protect them from wind and rain. They had little food and clothing. On the other hand, almost all the people of the world were disciples or lay supporters of brahmans. Therefore, even the Buddha was persecuted nine times. When the Buddha was passing the foot of Mount Gṛdhrakūṭa, Devadatta rolled a big stone down the slope at him. King Ajātaśatru turned an intoxicated elephant on the Buddha. King Ajita invited the Buddha and his disciples but did not offer them food, so they had to live on horses' oats for ninety days. In a city of brahmans, the Buddha and his disciples could get no food other than garbage. Ciñcā, the daughter of a brahman,

carried a tray under her garment and defamed the Buddha, saying that she was pregnant by him. Needless to say, the disciples of the Buddha were persecuted more. Many members of the Śākya clan were killed by King Virūḍhaka. Many of their attendants were trampled to death by intoxicated elephants. Utpalavarṇā Bhikṣuṇī was killed by Devadatta. Venerable Kālodāyin was put into a receptacle of horse dung. Venerable Maudgalyāyana was beaten to death with bamboo sticks.

Furthermore, the priests of the six Brahmanical sects came together to King Ajātaśatru and King Prasenajit and slandered the Buddha, saying:

> Gautama is the worst man in the Jambudvīpa. Wherever he comes, the three calamities and the seven difficulties occur. Just as the ocean swallows the waters of all rivers, or as a big mountain brings up all kinds of trees, Gautama collects many evil men such as Kāśyapa, Śāriputra, Maudgalyāyana, and Subhūti. One should be dutiful to his parents and loyal to his lord. The disciples of the Buddha are instigated by the Buddha. They do not follow the teachings of their parents. They renounce their families, violate the law promulgated by kings, and seclude themselves in mountains and forests. They should not remain in this country. Because they are here, the sun, the moon, and the stars become disordered, and many calamities take place on the earth.

This abuse was quite unbearable to the *śrāvaka*s. But the Buddha
218c also abused them as stated previously. The Buddha often criticized the *śrāvaka*s in the presence of great multitudes of gods and men. The *śrāvaka*s were quite at a loss as to what to do.

Furthermore, what troubled the *śrāvaka*s most was that the Buddha said to Subhūti in the *Vimalakīrtinirdeśa-sūtra,* "Those who give alms to you cannot be called fields of merit. Those who make offerings to you will fall into the three evil regions."

I will explain this in more detail. When the Buddha was at Āmravana, he said to a great multitude including Brahma, Śakra, the sun god, the moon god, the gods of the four quarters, the gods of the triple world, the gods of the earth, dragons, and others, "The gods and men who make offerings to Subhūti and other *bhikṣus* will fall into the three evil regions."

Do you think that the gods and men who heard this made offerings to these *śrāvakas*? It appears that the Buddha intended to starve adherents of the two vehicles to death. Some people may lose faith in the Buddha when they hear this. Adherents of the two vehicles may have been able to survive on the leftovers of food offered to the Buddha. Therefore, I have arrived at the following conclusion. If the Buddha had expounded only the sutras of the first forty and more years, and entered into *parinirvāṇa* without expounding the *Saddharmapuṇḍarīka-sūtra* during his last eight years, no one would make offerings to these venerables. These venerables might be living now in the region of hungry spirits [if they had not been saved by the *Saddharmapuṇḍarīka-sūtra*].

The Buddha said in the *Muryōgi-kyō,* "I have never revealed my true teaching during the past forty and more years," and denied the truthfulness of the sutras expounded previously, just as the spring sun melts away ice, or as a strong wind blows off the dew on the grass. He also says, "I will expound my true teaching only after a long period of expounding expedient teachings," which is as clear as a gale bringing forth black clouds, as the full moon shining in the sky, or as the sun shining in the cloudless sky. Then he assured Śāriputra, Kāśyapa, and others of Buddhahood, giving them Buddha names such as Padmaprabha Tathāgata and Raśmiprabhāsa Tathāgata. All these statements of the Buddha are clearly given in the sutra just as the sun or the moon shines brightly in the 219a
sky. These statements are given in the sutra only because those *śrāvakas* are worshiped like the Buddha by the followers among gods and men, after the extinction of the Tathāgata.

When the water is clear, the moon is reflected in it. When a strong wind blows, grasses and trees bend themselves before it. When the practitioner of the *Saddharmapuṇḍarīka-sūtra* appears, these saints should come to him, defying any difficulty, even passing through a great fire or a great rock.

[But the reality is that they have never come to protect me.] Kāśyapa entered into *samādhi,* vowing that he would do the work of the Buddha after the extinction of the Buddha. What is he doing now? I am very doubtful of him. Is this age not the fifth period of five centuries after the extinction of the Buddha? The Buddha said that the *Saddharmapuṇḍarīka-sūtra* would be propagated in the fifth period of five centuries after his extinction. Did he tell a lie? Am I not the practitioner of the *Saddharmapuṇḍarīka-sūtra*? Does the Buddha protect the great liars who say that their teachings have been handed down from the Buddha without resorting to written sutras, and who despise the *Saddharmapuṇḍarīka-sūtra* as one of the written sutras that do not express the true teachings of the Buddha? Does he protect those who tell people to give up, shut, desert, and abandon the *Saddharmapuṇḍarīka-sūtra,* and who have remodeled the Hokke-dō Hall [into the Amida-dō Hall]? The gods vowed to the Buddha that they would protect the practitioner of the *Saddharmapuṇḍarīka-sūtra*. Do they not come to protect me because they see the difficulties of this defiled world as too great to overcome? The sun and the moon are in the sky as usual. Mount Sumeru still stands unleveled. The tide rises and falls normally. The four seasons come and go regularly. Why is the practitioner of the *Saddharmapuṇḍarīka-sūtra* not protected as he should be? My doubts have become more and more serious.

Why Do the Bodhisattvas Not Protect Me?

Some great bodhisattvas, gods, and men were assured of their attainment of Buddhahood in the sutras expounded before the *Saddharmapuṇḍarīka-sūtra,* but that assurance did not materialize. It was only nominal, like a reflection of the moon in the water or like the shadow of a thing. A reflection of the moon has the form of the moon but not its substance. Therefore, the virtue of the Buddha who gave this nominal assurance was not as great as it seemed.

According to the *Avataṁsaka-sūtra,* when the World-honored One attained enlightenment, he kept silence without expounding the Dharma. Thereupon great bodhisattvas, more than sixty in number, including Dharma Wisdom Bodhisattva, Merits Forest Bodhisattva, Vajra Banner Bodhisattva, and Vajra Store Bodhisattva, came from the worlds of the ten quarters to the Lord Teacher Śākyamuni, the World-honored One. At the request of Gentle Face Bodhisattva, Emancipation Moon Bodhisattva, and others, they expounded the teachings of the ten periods, the ten practices, the ten turns, and the ten stages. These great bodhisattvas were not the disciples of Śākyamuni, the World-honored One. Brahmas and other gods of the worlds of the ten quarters 219b
also came and expounded the Dharma. These gods were not the disciples of Śākyamuni, the World-honored One, either. All the great bodhisattvas, gods, dragons, and others, who were among the congregation of the *Avataṁsaka-sūtra,* had already obtained inconceivable emancipation before Śākyamuni the World-honored One did. They may have been the disciples of Śākyamuni the World-honored One in his previous existence, or the disciples of the past Buddhas of the worlds of the ten quarters. They are not the disciples of the Buddha, the Lord Teacher, who attained enlightenment for the first time in this world.

The Buddha first obtained disciples when he expounded the four teachings [Hinayana teaching, Mahayana-cum-Hinayana teaching, Specialized Mahayana teaching, and Perfect Mahayana teaching] in the three periods: the period of the Āgama sutras, the period of the Vaipulya sutras, and the period of the Prajñāpāramitā sutras. But these teachings were not the true teachings of the Buddha. The Specialized Mahayana teaching and the Perfect Mahayana teaching were partially expounded in the periods of the Vaipulya sutras and Prajñāpāramitā sutras, but these teachings were not different from those expounded in the *Avataṁsaka-sūtra*. The *Avataṁsaka-sūtra* was in reality expounded by Dharma Wisdom Bodhisattva and other great bodhisattvas, not by the Lord Teacher Śākyamuni, the World-honored One. Therefore, we can say that these great bodhisattvas were the teachers of the Buddha, not the disciples of the Buddha as they seemed. Hearing the teachings of these great bodhisattvas, the World-honored One was so edified that he repeated those teachings in the periods of the Vaipulya sutras and Prajñāpāramitā sutras. Therefore, these great bodhisattvas are teachers of Śākyamuni. In the *Avataṁsaka-sūtra,* these great bodhisattvas are called "virtuous friends." A virtuous friend means a person who is not necessarily a teacher or a disciple.

The Hinayana teaching and the Mahayana-cum-Hinayana teaching derive from the Specialized Mahayana teaching and the Perfect Mahayana teaching. Therefore, those who understand the Specialized Mahayana teaching and the Perfect Mahayana teaching can easily understand the Hinayana teaching and the Mahayana-cum-Hinayana teaching.

A teacher is someone who tells his disciples what they do not
219c know. In India before the time of the Buddha, men, gods, and brahmans worshiped the two gods and respected the Three Seers as their teachers. Brahmanism was divided into ninety-five sects, but their views were not developed beyond the views of the Three Seers. The Lord Teacher, the World-honored One, at first studied Brahmanism. He was first a Brahmanist. After that he practiced asceticism as well as peaceful practices for twelve years, and then attained [the four truths:] the truth that all is suffering, the truth that all things are void, the truth that nothing is permanent, and the truth that nothing has a self-nature. Thereupon he ceased to be a Brahmanist. He called himself a man who obtained wisdom without teachers. Gods and men respectfully called him Great Teacher.

For the periods corresponding to the first four of the five tastes, the Lord Teacher Śākyamuni, the World-honored One, was a disciple of Dharma Wisdom Bodhisattva and other great bodhisattvas. The tradition that a bodhisattva was the teacher of the Buddha is also seen in the case of Mañjuśrī Bodhisattva, who is said to have been the teacher of the Buddha traced back to the ninth ancestry in the master-disciple lineage. That is why the Buddha said in many sutras, "I did not expound the Dharma even with a single letter [without restraint]."

The Buddha expounded the *Muryōgi-kyō* on Mount Sacred Eagle in the country of Magadha at the age of seventy-two. In this sutra he mentioned the names of the most important sutras he had expounded, and then said, "I have never expounded my true teaching during the past forty and more years."

Hearing this, great bodhisattvas, gods, and men were astonished. They asked the Buddha for his true teaching. The Buddha said one word but did not yet expound the Dharma. It reminds us of the moon emitting a ray of light from behind the eastern mountain to the western mountain without revealing itself to the eyes of the people.

At the beginning of the "Chapter on Expedients" in the *Saddharmapuṇḍarīka-sūtra,* the Buddha briefly expounded the teaching of one mind–three thousand, and thus for the first time he revealed what he had in his mind. The congregation was astonished to hear this, just as a half-asleep man is shocked at hearing a cuckoo chirp, or as on a fine day we see the rising moon as vaguely as if it were covered with thin clouds. Representing the gods, dragons, and great bodhisattvas, Śāriputra asked the Buddha, saying: 220a

> As many gods and dragons as there are sands in the Ganges River, and the eighty thousand bodhisattvas who are seeking Buddhahood, and also the wheel-turning holy kings of billions of worlds, are joining their hands together respectfully, wishing to hear the Perfect Way.

This statement means that Śāriputra wished to hear the teaching that he had never heard during the first forty and more years. The Buddha had expounded only the teachings corresponding to the first four of the five tastes, that is, only the first three of the four teachings, during the first forty-odd years.

"Wishing to hear the Perfect Way" can be explained as follows. It says in the *Mahāparinirvāṇa-sūtra,* "*Sa* means 'perfect.'" It says in the *Muemutoku-daijōshiron-gengi-ki* (*Wu-i-wute-ta-ch'eng-ssu-lun-hsüan-i-chi*), "*Sa* means 'six.'" The number six means perfect in India. It says in Chi-tsang's (Kichizō's) commentary, "*Sa* means 'perfect.'" It says in T'ien-t'ai's *Hokke-gengi* (*Fa-hua-hsüan-i*), Volume VIII, "*Sa* is a Sanskrit word. It is translated as 'wonderful.'"

Nāgārjuna Bodhisattva was the thirteenth patriarch. He founded the Shingon and Kegon Sects. He was the reincarnation of Dharma Cloud Freedom King Tathāgata. He was on the first of the ten stages of bodhisattvahood. He was a great saint. He wrote the *Mahāprajñāpāramitā-śāstra* compiled in a thousand volumes. He says in this writing, "*Sa* means 'six.'"

Myōhōrenge-kyō is [the Japanese pronunciation of] the title of a Chinese version of the *Saddharmapuṇḍarīka-sūtra*. It is called *Sattarumafundarikya-sotaran* in India.

The mantra at the core of the *Saddharmapuṇḍarīka-sūtra*, which Śubhākarasiṁha San-tsang found in an iron tower of South India, is as follows:

> *Nōmakusammandabodanan* (*namaḥ samyak sambuddhānām*), *on, a, an, aku* (*oṃ a aṁ aḥ*), *sarubaboda* (*sarvabuddhā*), *kino* (*jñā*), *sakishubiya* (*cakṣurbhyām*), *gyagyanōsanshaba* (*gagana saṁsvā*), *arakishani* (*rakṣaṇī*), *satsuridaruma fudarikya sotaran* (*saddharmapuṇḍarīka-sūtraṁ*), *ja, un, ban, koku* (*jā hūṃ ho*), *bazara rakishaman* (*vajra rakṣaman*), *un, sohaka* (*hūṁ svāhā*).

Satsuridaruma means the "right teaching." *Satsu* means "right." "Right" is "wonderful." "Wonderful" is "right." Hence, *Shōhoke-kyō* and *Myōhōrenge-kyō*. When *namu* (*namas*) is put before *Myōhōrenge-kyō*, it makes *Namu-myōhōrenge-kyō*.

Myō means "*go-soku.*" "Six" implies the six *pāramitā*s, which cover all practices. "Wishing to hear the Perfect Way" means "wishing to perfect the six *pāramitā*s." *Gu* means "to interpenetrate." It implies the truth that the ten regions interpenetrate one another. *Soku* means "to satisfy." It is satisfactory when one region interpenetrates the other nine regions. This sutra is compiled in eight

volumes, has twenty-eight chapters, and 69,384 characters. 220b
Every character is accompanied by the letter *myō,* and makes a Buddha by itself. The Buddha who is embodied in each character has the thirty-two major physical marks and the eighty minor physical marks. Each of the ten regions reveals the Buddha world in its own region. Miao-le says, "Since the living beings of each region have the fruits of Buddhahood, they also have the fruits of the natures of the living beings of the other nine regions."

The Buddha answered Śāriputra, saying, "The Buddhas appear in the worlds in order to cause all living beings to open the gate to the insight of the Buddha." Here "all living beings" include not only Śāriputra but also all living beings of the nine other regions and *icchantika*s.

Here the Buddha has fulfilled his vow to save all living beings. He says, "I once vowed that I would cause all living beings to become exactly as I am. That old vow of mine has now been fulfilled."

Hearing this, the great bodhisattvas and gods understood the words of the Buddha. They said:

> So far we have heard many teachings of the World-honored One. But we have never heard such a profound, wonderful and excellent teaching as this.

Dengyō Daishi comments on this, saying:

> "So far we have heard many teachings of the World-honored One" means that they have heard the great teachings expounded in the *Avataṁsaka-sūtra* and other sutras before the *Saddharmapuṇḍarīka-sūtra.* "We have never heard such a profound, wonderful, and excellent teaching as this" means that they have never heard the teaching that "there is only one Buddha vehicle," expounded in the *Saddharma-puṇḍarīka-sūtra.*
>
> They understood that the *Avataṁsaka-sūtra,* the Vaipulya sutras, the *Mahāprajñāpāramitā-sūtra,* the *Saṁdhinirmocana-sūtra,* the *Mahāvairocana-sūtra,* and other innumerable Mahayana sutras did not reveal the core

> of the teachings of the Buddha, the essence of the teaching of one mind–three thousand, that is to say, the two most important teachings: the possibility of the adherents of the two vehicles attaining Buddhahood and the eternity of Śākyamuni Buddha.

Now the great bodhisattvas, Brahma, Śakra, the sun god, the moon god, and the Heavenly Kings of the Four Quarters have become the disciples of the Lord Teacher Śākyamuni, the World-honored One. In the "Chapter on Beholding the Stupa of Treasures," the Buddha treated the great bodhisattvas as his disciples, and said, "Who will protect, keep, read, and recite this sutra after my extinction? Make a vow to do this before me!" The great
220c bodhisattvas followed the Buddha "just as the branches of trees bend and *kuśa* plants sway before a strong wind, or as the water of all rivers runs into the ocean."

At that time, however, the session on Mount Sacred Eagle was only halfway over [and the congregation could not understand the words of the Buddha very well]. They felt as if they were having a dream.

Thereupon the stupa of treasures appeared to prove the truthfulness of Śākyamuni's teachings. After that the Buddhas of the ten quarters assembled before the stupa of treasures, and Śākyamuni said that all these Buddhas were his emanations. Then Śākyamuni Buddha sat by the side of Prabhūtaratna in the stupa of treasures in the sky, and it was as if the sun and the moon were shining in the sky simultaneously. Gods and men were raised up into the sky and stayed there like the stars. Śākyamuni's Replica-Buddhas sat on the lion seats under the jeweled trees on the ground.

The universe as revealed in the *Avataṁsaka-sūtra* is called the Lotus Store world. In the Lotus Store world, the *sambhogakāya*s of the Buddhas of the worlds of the ten quarters as well as the *sambhogakāya* of Śākyamuni Buddha of this world stay in their own Buddha worlds. In other words, the Buddhas of the worlds of the ten quarters do not come to this Sahā world. They do not call themselves emanations of Śākyamuni Buddha. The Buddha of this world does not visit any of the worlds of the other Buddhas. The great bodhisattvas such as Dharma Wisdom Bodhisattva come to this world, but not the Buddhas.

It appears that the nine Honorable Ones on the eight petals of the lotus flower and the thirty-seven Honorable Ones as revealed in the *Mahāvairocana-sūtra* and the *Sarvatathāgatatattvasaṁgraha* are emanations of Mahāvairocana Tathāgata, but these emanations are not the beginningless Buddhas having the *trikāya*s. The one thousand Buddhas as revealed in the *Mahāprajñāpāramitā-sūtra* and the Buddhas of the worlds of the six quarters as revealed in the *Sukhāvatīvyūha-sūtra* did not come to this Sahā world. The Buddhas who assembled at the Great Treasure Hall as revealed in the *Mahāsaṃnipāta-sūtra* are not the emanations of Śākyamuni Buddha. The four Buddhas of the worlds of the four quarters as revealed in the *Suvarṇaprabhāsa* are the *nirmāṇakāya*s of the Buddha. In no sutra except the *Saddharmapuṇḍarīka-sūtra* did the Buddha collect the Buddhas provided with the *trikāya*s that they had obtained by their respective practices, and call them his emanations. Therefore, the "Chapter on Beholding the Stupa of Treasures" is an indirect introduction to the "Chapter on the Duration of the Life of the Tathāgata."

[In the "Chapter on Beholding the Stupa of Treasures,"] Śākyamuni, the World-honored One, who was still considered to have attained enlightenment forty-odd years before, collected the Buddhas who had attained enlightenment a kalpa or ten kalpas before and called them his emanations. This astonished the congregation because ranking the Buddhas into two, the Original Buddha and his emanations, is against the principle of equality. They thought that the Buddha who had attained enlightenment for the first time during his life in this world could not have disciples in the worlds of the ten quarters. Therefore, the Buddhas of the worlds of the ten quarters did not think that they had gained anything when they were called the emanations of Śākyamuni Buddha. T'ien-t'ai says, "The fact that Śākyamuni Buddha has so many Replica-Buddhas shows that he attained Buddhahood a long time ago." The congregation were astonished [because they had not yet been informed of the originality of Śākyamuni Buddha].

In addition to this, great bodhisattvas, as many as the par-
221a ticles of dust produced by pulverizing one thousand worlds, sprang up from underground. They were far more excellent in appearance than Samantabhadra and Mañjuśrī, both of whom were regarded as the most excellent disciples of Śākyamuni, the World-honored One. The great bodhisattvas who appeared in the *Avataṁsaka-sūtra,* the Vaipulya sutras, and the Prajñāpāramitā sutras, the great bodhisattvas who came to this Sahā world in the "Chapter on Beholding the Stupa of Treasures" of the *Saddharmapuṇḍarīka-sūtra,* and the sixteen great bodhisattvas including Vajrasattva of the *Mahāvairocana-sūtra,* were like monkeys or mountain-dwellers when compared with the great bodhisattvas from underground, who were like Śakra or noblemen.

Even Maitreya Bodhisattva, who was designated as the successor of Śākyamuni Buddha, did not know who they were. Needless to say, the other people did not know them, either. There were four great saints among these great bodhisattvas from underground: Viśiṣṭacāritra, Anantacāritra, Viśuddhacāritra, and Supratiṣṭhitacāritra. The bodhisattvas in the sky and on Mount Sacred Eagle could not see these four great saints squarely or think about them. The four bodhisattvas of the *Avataṁsaka-sūtra,* the four bodhisattvas of the *Mahāvairocana-sūtra,* and the sixteen great bodhisattvas of the *Sarvatathāgatatattvasaṁgraha* were like dim-sighted people before the sun, or like fishermen before the emperor, when they faced these four great saints. These four great saints were like the Four Saints headed by T'ai-kung-wang, or like the four grey-haired men (Ssu-hao, Shikō) of Mount Shang-shan (Shōzan), who attended Emperor Hui-ti (Keitei) of the Han dynasty. These four great saints were indeed that honorable. They were next to Śākyamuni, Prabhūtaratna, and the Replica-Buddhas of the worlds of the ten quarters. They should be respected as the virtuous friends of all living beings. Maitreya Bodhisattva thought:

> I have known all the bodhisattvas who appeared in this world and who have assembled here from the worlds of the ten quarters since the Buddha was a crown prince. Forty-two years ago, the Buddha attained enlightenment at the age of thirty. Now he is staying on Mount Sacred Eagle. I have visited the Pure Worlds as well as the defiled worlds of the ten quarters as a messenger of the Buddha or of my own will; therefore, I know the great bodhisattvas of those worlds. But I have never before seen any of the great bodhisattvas who have come from underground. Who is their teacher? Their teacher must be incomparably more excellent than Śākyamuni, Prabhūtaratna, or the Replica-Buddhas of the worlds of the ten quarters. When we see a
> heavy rain, we know that the dragon who caused the rain 221b
> is large. When we see a large lotus flower, we know that the pond is deep. I wonder what world they came from, what Buddha they met, and what teaching they learned.

He was too perplexed to say a word. Probably due to the power of the Buddha, however, he was able to ask the Buddha, saying:

> We have never before seen these many thousands of billions of bodhisattvas.... These bodhisattvas have great powers, virtue, and energy. Who expounded the Dharma to them? Who taught them? Who qualified them to attain perfect enlightenment? What teaching of the Buddha did they extol?... World-honored One! I have never seen them before. Tell me the name of the world in which they lived! I have visited many worlds, but have never seen them anywhere. I do not know any of them. They appeared suddenly from underground. Tell me why!

T'ien-t'ai says:

> Maitreya Bodhisattva meant to say, "During the period from the Buddha's attainment of enlightenment up to this session, many bodhisattvas have come here one after another from the worlds of the ten quarters. Their number is

> unlimited. I have seen and known all of them by the power of my wisdom by which I am designated as the successor of Śākyamuni Buddha. But I know none of these great bodhisattvas who have appeared from underground. I also have visited the worlds of the ten quarters and have seen the Buddhas there, and have been cordially introduced to the people there. But I have never seen these bodhisattvas from underground."

Miao-le says, "Only a wise man knows the origin of a thing. Only snakes know snakes." What is meant by the words of the sutra and Miao-le's comment on them is clear. It means that Maitreya Bodhisattva had never seen or heard of these bodhisattvas in this world, or in the worlds of the ten quarters since the Buddha's attainment of enlightenment.

The Buddha answered Maitreya, saying:

> Ajita! I know that you have never seen these... bodhisattvas. After I attained *anuttara-samyak-saṁbodhi* in the Sahā world, I taught these bodhisattvas, led them, trained them, and caused them to aspire to enlightenment.... I once sat under the bodhi tree in the city of Gayā, attained perfect enlightenment, and turned the wheel of the unsurpassed Dharma. I taught them, and caused them to aspire to enlightenment. Now they do not falter in seeking enlightenment.... I have been teaching them since the remotest past.

Thereupon Maitreya and other great bodhisattvas thought:

> DharmaWisdom Bodhisattva and many other great bodhisattvas joined the congregation of the *Avataṁsaka-sūtra*. We wondered who they were. The Buddha told us that they were his good friends of virtue. Therefore, our doubts were cleared. The same can be said of the great bodhisattvas who
> 221c joined the congregations at the Great Treasure Hall and the White Heron Pond. But these great bodhisattvas who have come from underground seem to be much older than those

> great bodhisattvas previously mentioned. We thought that they were the teachers of Śākyamuni, the World-honored One. But the Buddha says that he "caused them to aspire to enlightenment," and that he made these "young" people his disciples. This is quite unbelievable. Crown Prince Shōtoku of Japan was the son of the thirty-second Emperor Yōmei. When he was six years old, some old men came from Pekche, Kokuri, and China. The six-year-old Crown Prince said that they were his disciples. The old men joined their hands together toward him, and called him their teacher. This is unbelievable. There is the following story in China. A man saw on the roadside a young man about twenty years old beating an old man about eighty years old. He asked the young man why he beat the old man. The young man said that this old man was his son. [This is also unbelievable.] So is what the Buddha told us now.

Thereupon Maitreya Bodhisattva and others asked the Buddha, saying:

> World-honored One! When you, the Tathāgata, were a crown prince, you left the palace of the Śākyas, sat at the place of enlightenment not far from the city of Gayā, and attained *anuttara-samyak-saṁbodhi*. It is only forty-odd years since then. World-honored One! How did you do these great deeds of the Buddha in such a short time?

Bodhisattvas raised questions at every session of the Buddha's expounding of the Dharma during the forty-odd years since the time of his expounding of the *Avataṁsaka-sūtra*. The Buddha answered them and cleared the doubts of all living beings. But this question is probably the most difficult to answer. This is a far more difficult question than that raised by Great Adornment Bodhisattva and eighty thousand other bodhisattvas in the *Muryōgi-kyō:* How can one attain enlightenment instantly without the necessity of performing the bodhisattva practices for kalpas, which was required during the past forty and more years?

According to the *Kammuryōju-kyō* (*Kuan-wu-liang-shou-ching*), King Ajātaśatru imprisoned his father King Bimbisāra and usurped the throne at the instigation of Devadatta. He attempted to starve his father to death. Seeing this, his mother, Queen Vaidehī, carried food to the king in secret. The son tried to kill her, but released her on the advice of Jīvaka and Candraprabha.
222a The released queen invited the Buddha and asked him, "By what sin did I become the mother of this evil son? World-honored One! Why are you a relative of Devadatta?"

Her question was very important. She thought:

> The wheel-turning holy king is not born with his enemy. Śakra does not live with devils. The Buddha has been the Compassionate One for the past innumerable kalpas. Why is he living with his great enemy? Is he not the Buddha?

The Buddha did not answer her, however. Those who read and recite the *Kammuryōju-kyō* should read the "Chapter on Devadatta" in the *Saddharmapuṇḍarīka-sūtra*. Otherwise, this question will not be answered. The thirty-six questions raised by Kāśyapa Bodhisattva in the *Mahāparinirvāṇa-sūtra* are not as important as this question [raised by Maitreya Bodhisattva]. If the Buddha did not answer this question, all his teachings expounded throughout his life would be reduced to bubbles and all living beings would be caught in a mesh of doubts. The Buddha answered this question in the "Chapter on the Duration of the Life of the Tathāgata" in the *Saddharmapuṇḍarīka-sūtra*. This is why this chapter is the most important one.

The Buddha says in this chapter:

> The gods, men, and *asura*s in the world think that I, Śākyamuni Buddha, left the palace of the Śākyas, sat at the place of enlightenment not far from the city of Gayā, and attained *anuttara-samyak-saṁbodhi* [forty and more years ago].

This statement expresses the thought of all the great bodhisattvas and others who have heard the Buddha from the time that the

Avataṁsaka-sūtra was expounded at the place of enlightenment up to the time of his expounding the "Chapter on Peaceful Practices" in the *Saddharmapuṇḍarīka-sūtra.*

The Buddha goes on to say, "To tell the truth, good men, it is many hundreds of thousands of billions of *nayuta*s of kalpas since I became the Buddha."

This means that the following [eight] statements are false:

1. It is stated as many as three times in the *Avataṁsaka-sūtra* that the Buddha attained enlightenment for the first time during his life in this world.

2. The Āgama sutras also contain the same statement.

3. It says in the *Vimalakīrtinirdeśa-sūtra* that the Buddha sat under the tree for the first time during his life in this world.

4. The *Mahāsaṁnipāta-sūtra* reads that it is sixteen years since the Tathāgata attained enlightenment.

5. It says in the *Mahāvairocana-sūtra* that the Buddha first sat at the place of enlightenment during his life in this world.

6. It says in the *Ninnō-hannya-kyō* that the Buddha has been expounding the Dharma for the past twenty-nine years.

7. It says in the *Muryōgi-kyō* that the Buddha sat at the place of enlightenment under the tree for six years.

8. In the "Chapter on Expedients" in the *Saddharma-puṇḍarīka-sūtra,* the Buddha says that he sat at the place of enlightenment for the first time during his life in this world.

All these statements of the Buddha now turn out to be false. Here the beginninglessness of the life of the Buddha is revealed, and all the Buddhas have become the emanations of Śākyamuni, the World-honored One.

In the first fourteen chapters of the *Saddharmapuṇḍarīka-sūtra* as well as in the earlier sutras, Śākyamuni, the World-honored One, stood equal to the other Buddhas. Buddhas practice 222b
differently. Therefore, those who worshiped a particular Buddha

other than Śākyamuni despised Śākyamuni. But now Vairocana Buddha on the lotus flower of the *Avataṁsaka-sūtra,* and the Buddhas who appeared in the Vaipulya sutras, the Prajñā-pāramitā sutras, and the *Mahāvairocana-sūtra* have become the followers of Śākyamuni.

The Buddha attained enlightenment at the age of thirty and became the lord of the Sahā world, replacing the Great Brahma Heavenly King and the God of the Sixth Heaven. In the first fourteen chapters of the *Saddharmapuṇḍarīka-sūtra* and in the earlier sutras, the Buddha called the worlds of the ten quarters the Pure Worlds of the Buddhas, and despised the Sahā world as a defiled world. Now this world has become the world of the Original Buddha, and the Pure Worlds of the ten quarters have become the defiled worlds of the emanations of the Original Buddha. Since the Buddha is eternal, the great bodhisattvas who have appeared in the first fourteen chapters of the *Saddharma-puṇḍarīka-sūtra* and the bodhisattvas of the other worlds have become the disciples of the Lord Teacher Śākyamuni, the World-honored One. Without the "Chapter on the Duration of the Life of the Tathāgata," all the sutras would be like the sky without the sun and the moon, like a country without a king, like mountains and rivers without gems, or like a man without a soul.

However, in order to praise the sutras they prefer, Ch'eng-kuan, Chia-shang, Tz'u-en, Kōbō, and other wise-appearing teachers of the Provisional Mahayana sects, such as Kegon and Shingon, say that the Lord Teacher of the *Avataṁsaka-sūtra* is the *sambhogakāya* while the Lord Teacher of the *Saddharma-puṇḍarīka-sūtra* is the *nirmāṇakāya,* or that the Buddha in the "Chapter on the Duration of the Life of the Tathāgata" in the *Saddharmapuṇḍarīka-sūtra* is still at the stage of darkness while the Buddha of the *Mahāvairocana-sūtra* is at the stage of brightness. Clouds hide the moon. Slanderous vassals conceal wise men. When praised, a yellow stone looks like a gem, and a flatterer appears to be a wise man. Now the scholars of this defiled world are deceived by them and do not treasure the gem of the "Chapter on the Duration of the Life of the Tathāgata." The teachers of the Tendai Sect also are deceived by them, and think that gold is the same as a stone.

If the Buddha is not eternal, his disciples will be few. The moon does not begrudge making its reflection, but it cannot reflect itself without water. The Buddha wishes to teach people, but it would be useless for him to complete the eight aspects of his life without people. The *śrāvaka*s were assured of their attainment of Buddhahood in the first fourteen chapters of the *Saddharmapuṇḍarīka-sūtra,* but they did not become Buddhas at once. They were allowed only to proceed to the first of the ten stages, or to the first of the ten periods of bodhisattva practices, because they were too preoccupied with saving themselves to be able to save others before the *Saddharmapuṇḍarīka-sūtra* was expounded. They had 222c
to complete the eight aspects of the Buddha in their future lives.

Brahma, Śakra, the sun god, the moon god, and the Heavenly Kings of the Four Quarters have now become the disciples of the Buddha. As far as the first fourteen chapters of the *Saddharmapuṇḍarīka-sūtra* are concerned, however, the Lord Teacher Śākyamuni, the World-honored One, attained enlightenment only forty-odd years before, while the gods had been ruling this world from the beginning of the kalpa of composition. Therefore, although the hearers of the *Saddharmapuṇḍarīka-sūtra,* expounded during eight years on Mount Sacred Eagle, understood that the Buddha is the teacher of the gods, they were still attracted by the gods, just as a newly enthroned king is not as popular as the retired king.

Since the eternity of Śākyamuni Buddha has been revealed, Sūryaprabhāsana and Candraprabha, accompanying Bhaiṣajyaguru Tathāgata in the west; the disciples of the Buddhas of the worlds of the ten quarters; and the great bodhisattvas who are the disciples of Mahāvairocana Tathāgata of the two *dhātu*s, revealed in the *Mahāvairocana-sūtra,* the *Sarvatathāgatatattva-saṁgraha,* and other sutras; have become the disciples of the Lord Teacher Śākyamuni, the World-honored One. Since the Buddhas are the emanations of Śākyamuni Tathāgata, their disciples are also the disciples of Śākyamuni Tathāgata. Needless to say, the sun god, the moon god, the star gods, and the other gods who have been living in this world from the beginning of the kalpa of composition of this world have become the disciples of the Lord Teacher Śākyamuni, the World-honored One.

Sects other than the Tendai Sect worship the wrong Buddha as the Most Honorable One. The Kusha, Jōjitsu, and Ritsu Sects worship Śākyamuni, the World-honored One, who attained enlightenment by eliminating thirty-four illusions. Here the Buddha lowers his own dignity, just as when a crown prince thinks that he is the son of a commoner. The Kegon, Shingon, Sanron, and Hossō Sects are Mahayana sects. The Hossō and Sanron Sects worship the Buddha resembling the superior *nirmāṇakāya* as the Most Honorable One. Here the Buddha degrades himself, just as when a crown prince thinks that he is the son of a guardsman. The Kegon and Shingon Sects despise Śākyamuni, the World-honored One, and worship Vairocana and Mahāvairocana respectively. Here Śākyamuni is replaced by a religious king of obscure origin, just as when a king is replaced by a person of suspicious identity. The Jōdo Sect abandons the Lord Teacher and worships Amitābha Buddha, who is an emanation of Śākyamuni, on the belief that Amitābha is the Buddha associated with the living beings of this world. The Zen Sect despises both the Buddha and the sutras expounded by the Buddha, just as an arrogant son despises his
223a parents. All this comes from their ignorance about the Most Honorable One.

The people who were born before the time of the three Huang emperors were like beasts because they did not know their fathers. Just like them, the teachers of those sects are like beasts because they do not know the "Chapter on the Duration of the Life of the Tathāgata." They do not know the favors given by others. Miao-le says:

> Throughout all the sutras expounded by the Buddha, the eternity of the Buddha is not revealed anywhere else than

> in the "Chapter on the Duration of the Life of the Tathāgata." We should know the duration of the lives of our parents. If we do not know the duration of the life of the Buddha, who is our father, we shall not be able to know his Pure World. The teachers of these sects are clever but inhuman because they do not know that they should be dutiful to their father, that is, the Buddha.

Miao-le Ta-shih was active in the years of T'ien-pao (Tempō) at the end of the T'ang dynasty. He carefully studied the teachings of the Sanron, Kegon, Hossō, and Shingon Sects and their sutras, and said that those who do not know the Buddha revealed in the "Chapter on the Duration of the Life of the Tathāgata" are clever beasts because they are ignorant of the Pure World of the Eternal Buddha. "Clever but inhuman" means that Fa-tsang of the Kegon Sect and Śubhākarasiṁha of the Shingon Sect were clever but did not know the fatherhood of the Buddha just like a son who does not know his father.

Dengyō Daishi was the founder of Exoteric Buddhism and also of the Esoteric Buddhism of Japan. He says in his *Hokke-shūku:*

> In the sutras of sects other than the Tendai Hokke Sect, the Buddha's motherly love is expounded rather than his fatherly strictness. The Tendai Hokke Sect expounds both his motherly love and his fatherly strictness. According to the Tendai Hokke Sect, the Buddha is the father of all the saints and sages, of the *śrāvaka*s who have something more to learn, of the *śrāvaka*s who have nothing more to learn, and of those who have begun to aspire to enlightenment.

The sutras of the Shingon and Kegon Sects do not mention even the names of the three steps of emanation: (1) to sow the seed of Buddhahood, (2) to grow the plant of Buddhahood, and (3) to develop Buddhahood into emancipation. Needless to say, those sutras do not explain these three steps.

The sutras of the Kegon and Shingon Sects make the statement that we shall be able to proceed to the first of the ten stages of enlightenment during our life in this world and then become Buddhas. Those sutras are, however, the sutras of Provisional Mahayana teachings; therefore, they do not mention the seed of Buddhahood. Emancipation without knowing the seed of Buddhahood sown in one's own mind is fruitless, just as Ch'ao-kao (Chōkō) or Dōkyō, who had no royal blood, failed to usurp the throne. All the sects criticize one another, but I do not do so. I only depend on the *Saddharmapuṇḍarīka-sūtra.*

Vasubandhu Bodhisattva discovered the seed of Buddhahood implicitly expounded in the *Saddharmapuṇḍarīka-sūtra* and said that the most important thing is to know the seed of Buddhahood. The seed of Buddhahood is explained in T'ien-t'ai's teaching of one mind–three thousand. According to T'ien-t'ai, the seeds of the various honorable ones given in the *Avataṁsaka-sūtra,* the *Mahāvairocana-sūtra,* and other Mahayana sutras come from the seed of Buddhahood. The teaching of one mind–three thousand was established by T'ien-t'ai Chih-che Ta-shih (Tendai Chisha Daishi) and no one else.

Ch'eng-kuan of the Kegon Sect took the teaching of one mind–three thousand from T'ien-t'ai and utilized it to interpret the *Avataṁsaka-sūtra*'s statement, "The mind is like a skillful painter." The possibility of attaining Buddhahood by adherents of the two vehicles, the eternity of the life of Śākyamuni Buddha, and the teaching of one mind–three thousand are not found in the *Mahāvairocana-sūtra* or other sutras of the Shingon Sect. Śubhākarasiṁha San-tsang came to China, read T'ien-t'ai's *Makashikan,* and gained a new understanding. He appropriated the teaching of one mind–three thousand from T'ien-t'ai, using it to interpret "the reality of the mind" and "I am the origin of all," as stated in the
223b *Mahāvairocana-sūtra.* Thus he made the teaching of one mind–three thousand the basis of the Shingon Sect. Furthermore, he added mudras and mantras to the teaching, and said that the *Mahāvairocana-sūtra* and the *Saddharmapuṇḍarīka-sūtra* are the same in theory, but that the *Mahāvairocana-sūtra* is superior to the *Saddharmapuṇḍarīka-sūtra* because the former has mudras and mantras. He said that the mandalas of the two *dhātu*s

demonstrate the teachings of the possibility of attaining Buddhahood by adherents of the two vehicles and the mutual interpenetration of the ten regions. Is there any mention of these two teachings in the *Mahāvairocana-sūtra*? Śubhākarasiṁha's statement is most deceptive. Therefore, Dengyō Daishi says:

> The newly imported Shingon Sect ignores the transmission of the Dharma by I-hsing (Ichigyō) of the Tendai Sect. The earlier imported Kegon Sect conceals the views of its own sect due to the influence of the Tendai Sect.

The famous tanka poem, "*Honobono to. . . ,*" was composed by Hitomaro. But if you go to a remote island and tell the islanders that you wrote that poem, they may believe you. The same can be said of the scholars of China and Japan, who make such deceptive statements as this.

Liang-hsü Ho-shang (Ryōsho Oshō) says, "The Shingon, Zen, Kegon, and Sanron Sects are introductory to the *Saddharmapuṇḍarīka-sūtra.*" Śubhākarasiṁha San-tsang once fell seriously ill. In a coma, he dreamed that he was sent to the afterworld and tortured by Yama because he had abandoned the *Saddharmapuṇḍarīka-sūtra*. After he awoke from the dream, he had faith in the *Saddharmapuṇḍarīka-sūtra* and was released from the torture.

Śubhākarasiṁha, Amoghavajra, and others place the *Saddharmapuṇḍarīka-sūtra* in the center of each of the two mandalas like a great king, and put on the sides of the sutra the *Mahāvairocana-sūtra* of the *garbhadhātu* and the *Sarvatathāgatatattvasaṁgraha* of the *vajradhātu* like two ministers accompanying the great king. Kōbō Daishi of Japan did the same when he transmitted the way of the practices of the Shingon Sect to Jitsu-e, Shinga, Encho, and Kōjō, although due to the influence of the Kegon Sect, he regarded the *Saddharmapuṇḍarīka-sūtra* as only the third most important sutra.

Chia-hsiang (Kajō) of the Sanron Sect said in his *Hokke-genron* (*Fa-hua-hsüan-lun*) compiled in ten volumes:

> The *Saddharmapuṇḍarīka-sūtra* was expounded in the fourth period [the period of the Prajñāpāramitā sutras]. In this sutra, the two vehicles are criticized and then reappropriated and merged into the Buddha vehicle.

But he later followed T'ien-t'ai and "stopped lecturing, dismissed his congregation, and made himself a footstep for T'ien-t'ai who was going up to the elevated lecture seat." Thus he served T'ien-
223c t'ai for seven years.

Tz'u-en of the Hossō Sect said in his *Hō-on-girinjō* (*Fa-yüan-i-lin-chang*) compiled in seven volumes, "The One Vehicle is an expedient teaching. The three vehicles are the true teaching of the Buddha," and many other wrong views. But in the *Hokke-genzan-yōshū* (*Fa-hua-hsüan-tsan-yao-chi*), Volume IV, written by his disciple Ch'i-fu (Saifuku), it says that the true intention of Tz'u-en was to put his sect into the group of indefinite teachings by admitting the views of both the Kegon and Tendai Sects. This view is ambiguous, but it implies that he followed T'ien-t'ai in his heart.

Ch'eng-kuan of the Kegon Sect said in his commentary on the *Avataṁsaka-sūtra* that the *Saddharmapuṇḍarīka-sūtra* is a sutra of expedient teachings when compared with the *Avataṁsaka-sūtra,* but he also said:

> The Tendai Sect says that the teaching of one mind–three thousand is the true teaching of the Buddha. This teaching is not inconsistent with the teaching of the Kegon Sect.

Doesn't this statement mean that he repented of his statement that the *Saddharmapuṇḍarīka-sūtra* is a sutra of expedient teachings?

The same can be said of Śubhākarasiṁha and Kōbō. We cannot see our faces without a mirror. We cannot discover our own faults without our enemies. The scholars of the Shingon and other sects did not know their own faults. I think that when they saw Dengyō Daishi, they realized the defects of their sects.

It says in some sutras expounded before the *Saddharma-puṇḍarīka-sūtra* that a certain bodhisattva, a man or a god, attained Buddhahood. Their attainment of Buddhahood was not real but fabulous because the vow of Śākyamuni and the other Buddhas to save all living beings was not fulfilled in any other sutra until the *Saddharmapuṇḍarīka-sūtra,* in which the Buddha said, "I once vowed that I would cause all living beings to become exactly as I am. That old vow of mine has now been fulfilled."

Therefore, I can say this. Those who study and practice the *Avataṁsaka-sūtra,* the *Kammuryōju-kyō,* the *Mahāvairocana-sūtra,* and other sutras will undoubtedly be protected by the Buddhas, bodhisattvas, and gods of those sutras. But if they oppose a practitioner of the *Saddharmapuṇḍarīka-sūtra,* their protectors will leave them and protect the practitioner of the *Saddharmapuṇḍarīka-sūtra* instead.

A dutiful son will leave his father and follow the king if his father becomes an enemy of the king. It is the true virtue of filial piety to do so. The same can be said of the teachings of the Buddha. I shall be protected not only by the Buddhas, bodhisattvas, and the ten *rākṣasīs* of the *Saddharmapuṇḍarīka-sūtra* but also by the Buddhas of the worlds of the six quarters and twenty-five bodhisattvas of the Jōdo Sect, the one thousand two hundred honorable ones of the Shingon Sect, and the honorables and guardian 224a
gods of the seven sects, just as Dengyō Daishi was protected by the guardian gods of the seven sects.

I thought that if the practitioner of the *Saddharmapuṇḍarīka-sūtra* appeared, the sun god, the moon god, and other gods, who attended at the three sessions of the two places of the *Saddharma-puṇḍarīka-sūtra,* would immediately come to him just as a magnet attracts iron or as the moon reflects itself on the water, and fulfill their vow to protect him. But they have not yet come to me. Am I not the practitioner of the *Saddharmapuṇḍarīka-sūtra*? I will consult sutras again and see whether I am wrong or not in saying this.

Chapter III

The Five Testimonies to the Truthfulness of My Faith

The First Testimony

Question: Why do you say that the priests of the Nembutsu and Zen Sects are enemies of the *Saddharmapuṇḍarīka-sūtra* and that they are evil friends of all living beings?

Answer: I have no intention of expressing my own opinion. I will just quote from sutras and commentaries on the sutras. The sutras and commentaries will be a mirror that reflects the ugly faces of the slanderers of the Dharma, and shows us their faults. You will be able to see their faults unless you are blind from birth.

It says in the "Chapter on Beholding the Stupa of Treasures" in the *Saddharmapuṇḍarīka-sūtra,* Volume IV:

> Thereupon Many Treasures Buddha in the stupa of treasures offered half of his seat to Śākyamuni Buddha.... The great multitude saw the two Tathāgatas sitting cross-legged on the lion seat in the stupa of the seven treasures.... Śākyamuni Buddha ... said to the four kinds of devotees [monks, nuns, laymen, and laywomen] in a loud voice, "Who will expound the *Sutra of the Lotus Flower of the Wonderful Dharma* in this Sahā world? Now is the time to do this. I shall enter into nirvana before long. I wish to transmit the *Sutra of the Lotus Flower of the Wonderful Dharma* to someone so that this sutra may be preserved."

This is the first testimony to the truthfulness of my faith.

The Second Testimony

It also says in the same chapter:

> Thereupon the World-honored One, wishing to repeat what he had said, sang in *gāthās*, "The Saintly Master, the World-honored One, who had passed away a long time ago, came riding in the stupa of treasures to hear the Dharma direct from me. Could anyone who sees him not make efforts to hear the Dharma?... The Replica-Buddhas as innumerable as there are sands in the Ganges River also came here from their wonderful worlds, parting from their disciples, and giving up the offerings made to them by gods, men, and dragons, in order to hear the Dharma... and to have the Dharma preserved forever.... Wonderful fragrance is sent forth from the bodies of those Buddhas to the worlds of the ten quarters. The living beings of those worlds smell the fragrance joyfully just as the branches of a tree bend before a strong wind. Those Buddhas employ these expedients in order to have the Dharma preserved forever." [The Buddha said to the great multitude,] "Who will protect, keep, read, and recite this sutra after my extinction? Make a vow be-
> 224b fore me to do this!"

This is the second testimony to the truthfulness of my faith.

The Third Testimony

It goes on to say:

> Many Treasures Tathāgata and I, and the Replica-Buddhas who have assembled here, wish to know who will do all this.... Good men! Think this over clearly! It is difficult to expound this sutra. Make a great vow to do this! It is not difficult to expound all the other sutras, as many as there are sands in the Ganges River. It is not difficult to grasp Mount Sumeru and hurl it to a distance of countless

> Buddha worlds.... It is difficult to expound this sutra in the evil world after my extinction.... It is not difficult to shoulder a load of hay and stay unburned in the fire at the end of the kalpa of destruction. It is difficult to keep this sutra and expound it to even one person after my extinction.... Good men! Who will keep, read, and recite this sutra after my extinction? Make a vow before me to do all this!

This is the third testimony to the truthfulness of my faith. The fourth and fifth testimonies will be quoted from the "Chapter on Devadatta," as you will see later.

The meaning of these three testimonies is as clear as the sun in the blue sky or as moles on a white face. But it is difficult for a blind-born, squint-eyed, or one-eyed man, or one who thinks that his teacher is the wisest, or a prejudiced man, to understand it. Therefore, to those who seek enlightenment, I will explain it in more detail no matter how much I may be persecuted for doing so.

[It is very difficult to meet the true teaching of the Buddha.] It is more difficult than it is for the peach plants of Queen Hsi-wang-mu (Sei-ō-bo) to bear fruit or for the *udumbara* flowers of the wheel-turning holy king to bloom.

[History tells us that there were heated controversies between the propagators of the true teaching of the Buddha and those who did not know the true teaching of the Buddha.] In China, F'ei-kung fought with Hsiang-yü (Kō-u) for eight years. In Japan, Yoritomo fought with Munemori for seven years. *Asura*s fought with Śakra. *Garuḍa*s fought with dragons at the Anavatapta Pond. But these fights were not so severe [as the controversies between the advocates of the *Saddharmapuṇḍarīka-sūtra* and the slanderers of it].

You should know that the true teaching of the Buddha has been revealed twice in Japan, at the time of Dengyō Daishi and at this time of Nichiren. Men of no eyes may doubt this. That cannot be helped. I believe that the above-mentioned three testimonies show that Śākyamuni, Prabhūtaratna, and the Buddhas of the worlds of the ten quarters assembled and determined the ranking in value of all the sutras propagated in Japan, China, India, the palaces of dragons, heaven, and the worlds of the ten quarters.

Question: [In the third testimony, the expression "difficult" is repeated six times in connection with the keeping of this sutra, and the expression "not difficult" is repeated nine times in connection with doing other things. Therefore, we can say that there are two kinds of sutras, the sutras of six difficulties and the sutras of nine easinesses.] Are the *Avataṁsaka-sūtra,* the Vaipulya sutras, the *Mahāprajñāpāramitā-sūtra,* the *Saṁdhinirmocana-sūtra,* the *Laṅkāvatāra-sūtra,* the *Mahāvairocana-*
224c *sūtra,* and the *Mahāparinirvāṇa-sūtra* among the sutras of nine easinesses or among the sutras of six difficulties?

Answer: The teachers of the Kegon Sect who had the title of San-tsang or Ta-shih conferred on them, such as Tu-shun, Chih-yen, Fa-tsang, and Ch'eng-kuan, read this part of the sutra and said that the *Saddharmapuṇḍarīka-sūtra* and the *Avataṁsaka-sūtra* are among the sutras of six difficulties and that both sutras are the same in purpose and theory, just as the four theories—(1) the truth that everything exists, (2) the truth that nothing exists, (3) the truth that everything exists while nothing exists, and (4) the truth that both the truth that everything exists and the truth that nothing exists are negative—lead us to one and the same truth.

Hsüan-tsang San-tsang and Tz'u-en Ta-shih of the Hossō Sect say that both the *Saṁdhinirmocana-sūtra* and the *Saddharmapuṇḍarīka-sūtra* expound the teaching of the Yuishiki (Vijñaptimātra) [or Hossō] Sect, and that the two sutras were expounded in the last of the three periods of the teaching of the Buddha, and accordingly, that the two sutras are among the sutras of six difficulties.

Chi-tsang (Kichizō) and others of the Sanron Sect say that the *Mahāprajñāpāramitā-sūtra* and the *Saddharmapuṇḍarīka-sūtra* are identical to each other in content, and expound one and the same teaching.

Śubhākarasiṁha San-tsang, Vajrabodhi San-tsang, and Amoghavajra San-tsang say that the *Mahāvairocana-sūtra* is equal to the *Saddharmapuṇḍarīka-sūtra* in theory, and that both sutras are among the sutras of six difficulties. Kōbō of Japan says:

> The *Mahāvairocana-sūtra* is not a sutra of six difficulties or of nine easinesses. It was not expounded by Śākyamuni. It was expounded by the *dharmakāya* of Mahāvairocana Tathāgata.

Some say that the *Avataṁsaka-sūtra* was expounded by the *sambhogakāya,* and therefore that it is not a sutra of six difficulties or of nine easinesses.

The founders and other teachers of these four sects had these views. Thousands of students who follow them today do not go beyond the views of their predecessors.

I lament all this. If I criticize these teachers, the people of today will shun me. They will do more and more wrongs to me. They will finally slander me before the government, and I shall be killed. But our Compassionate Father said on his deathbed between the two trees, "Depend on the Dharma, not on a person!" "A person" means any of the four kinds of persons on whom people can depend for a peaceful life. "Do not depend on a person" means that we should not listen even to those bodhisattvas equal to Buddhas, such as Samantabhadra or Mañjuśrī, unless they expound the Dharma carrying sutras in their hands. The Buddha also says, "Depend on a sutra in which a teaching is thoroughly expounded, not on a sutra in which the expounding of a teaching is not completed!" We should believe and receive a sutra after we see that the sutra completely expounds a teaching. It says in Nāgārjuna Bodhisattva's *Daśabhūmivibhāṣā-śāstra,* "A theory not based on sutras is wrong. A theory based on sutras is right." 225a
T'ien-t'ai Ta-shih says, "A theory consistent with sutras should be recorded for use. We should not believe or receive a theory which is not mentioned or implied in sutras." Dengyō Daishi says, "Depend on the words of the Buddha, not on oral instructions of

persons other than the Buddha!" Enchin Chicho Daishi says, "Transmit the Dharma according to the words of the sutra!"

It appears that these teachers determined the value of a theory according to the words of sutras and *śāstras*, but the reality is that they clung to their own sects and did not rectify the faults of their predecessors. Therefore, their evaluation of a theory was just a product of their distortion and prejudice, and their teaching is for the purpose of defending their own views.

The Vātsīputrīya and the Vaipulya Sects after the extinction of the Buddha were more spiteful and more cunning in argumentation than Brahmanism before the Buddha. Confucians after the Later Han dynasty were also more so than in the time of the three Huang emperors and the five Ti emperors. Because the priests of the Kegon, Hossō, and Shingon Sects are jealous of the true teachings of the Tendai Sect, they ever more persistently "distort the meaning of the sutra of True Mahayana and utilize it to justify the sutra of Provisional Mahayana." Those who wish to attain the enlightenment of the Buddha should abandon prejudice, refrain from controversies between sects, and not despise persons of the other sects.

The Buddha says in the *Saddharmapuṇḍarīka-sūtra:*

> I have expounded many sutras. I am now expounding this sutra. I will also expound many sutras in the future.... This *Sutra of the Lotus Flower of the Wonderful Dharma* is the most difficult to believe and the most difficult to understand.

This means that the *Saddharmapuṇḍarīka-sūtra* is the most excellent of all the sutras ever expounded, being expounded, or to be expounded.

Miao-le says:

> Some sutras have the statement, "This is the king of all sutras." But none of them has the statement, "This is the most excellent of all the sutras ever expounded, being expounded, or to be expounded...." Those who slander the most excellent

> of all the sutras ever expounded, being expounded, or to be expounded will suffer in hell for many kalpas.

I was astonished to find these words of the sutra and this commentary on them. I studied many sutras and also commentaries written by various scholars, and finally my doubts have been cleared. The foolish priests of the Shingon Sect of today treasure mudras and mantras, and follow Jikaku Daishi and others who say that the Shingon Sect is superior to the sect of the *Saddharmapuṇḍarīka-sūtra*. The words of those Shingon people are not worth noting.

It says in the *Ghanavyūha-sūtra:*

> The *Jūji-kyō* (*Shih-ti-ching*), *Avataṁsaka-sūtra*, *Daiju-kinnara-kyō* (*Ta-shu-chin-na-lo-ching*), *Jinzū-kyō* (*Shen-t'ung-ching*), *Śrīmālāsiṁhanāda-sūtra,* and other sutras come from this sutra. This *Ghanavyūha-sūtra* is the most excellent of all the sutras.

It says in the *Daiun-kyō* (*Ta-yü-ching*):

> This sutra is the wheel-turning holy king of all the sutras because the Dharma store[house], including the true nature of all living beings, the Buddha-nature of all living beings, and the eternity of all living beings, is expounded in this sutra.

It says in the *Ropparamitsu-kyō* (*Liu-po-lo-mi-ching*):

> The right teachings expounded by the innumerable Buddhas in the past, and the eighty-four thousand wonderful teach- 225b
> ings which I am expounding now, are composed of the five storehouses: (1) Sutra, (2) Vinaya, (3) Abhidharma, (4) Prajñāpāramitā sutras, and (5) *Dhāraṇīs*. The Buddha teaches all living beings with these five storehouses. To those who cannot receive the first four storehouses, or to those who have committed the four grave sins, the eight grave sins, or the five hell-bound sins, or to the *icchantika*s who have slandered the Mahayana sutras, the Buddhas expound

the storehouse of *dhāraṇīs* in order to have them expiate their grave sins, to emancipate themselves from suffering quickly, and to attain nirvana instantly. These five storehouses of the Dharma are like the five tastes of milk: fresh milk, cream, curdled milk, butter, and ghee. *Dhāraṇīs* can be likened to ghee, which is the most wonderful taste. *Dhāraṇīs* can eliminate all diseases, and give peace of mind and body to all living beings. *Dhāraṇīs* are the most excellent storehouse of the Dharma. *Dhāraṇīs* cause all living beings to expiate their grave sins.

It says in the *Saṁdhinirmocana-sūtra:*

Thereupon Superior Truth-Born Bodhisattva said to the Buddha again:

"World-honored One! At Śāraṅganātha Grove in the city of Vārāṇasī, you for the first time turned the wheel of the Dharma in the form of the Four Noble Truths for those who sought the *śrāvaka* vehicle. The teaching was very strange and rare to hear because it had never been expounded by any god or man in the world before. But there was something more to be added to it. The teaching was not yet final. There was room for further discussion.

"World-honored One! In the second period of your teaching, you implicitly turned the wheel of the Dharma for those who aspired to the Great Vehicle with the teaching that nothing has its own nature, that nothing is born or extinguished, that all things are calm and tranquil from the outset, and that all things are nirvana by themselves. This teaching was more strange and rarer to hear than the teaching expounded in the first period. But there was something more to be added to it. This teaching was not yet final. There was room for further discussion.

"World-honored One! Now in the third [and last] period of your teaching, you have explicitly turned the wheel of the Dharma for those who aspire to the vehicle of all living beings with the teaching that nothing has its own nature, that nothing is born or extinguished, that all things are calm and tranquil from the outset, that all things are nirvana by themselves, and that there is no nature that can be called the nature of a thing. This teaching is the most strange and rarest to hear. Now the wheel of the Dharma turned by you, the World-honored One, has no more excellent teaching. Nothing more is to be added to it. This teaching is final. There is no room for further discussion."

It says in the *Mahāprajñāpāramitā-sūtra:*

Those who have *prajñā* can skillfully enter the profound truth, that is, the Dharma-nature, by hearing any teaching, spiritual or secular. Those who do secular things with 225c
prajñā can enter the Dharma-nature. They see nothing that is not the Dharma-nature.

It says in the *Mahāvairocana-sūtra,* Volume I:

[Mahāvairocana, the World-honored One, said to Vajrapāṇi, the Master of Mystery:]

"Master of Mystery! There is a practice of the Great Vehicle. It is to see that nothing exists outside the mind. Nothing has its own self. Why is that? It is because one who performed this practice saw that the *ālaya-vijñāna* [storehouse consciousness] was like a phantom.... Master of Mystery! By this practice, he was able to abandon the conception of self, obtain freedom of mind, and realize that from the very beginning his mind had never been born.... The so-called emptiness of the mind means that the mind is free from the sense organs and sense objects, and that it is empty of form and realms, that it transcends fruitless discussions about relativities, and it is like the sky.... It is the perfect state of non-self."

Mahāvairocana, the World-honored One, said to the Master of Mystery, "Master of Mystery! What is *bodhi?*"

The Master of Mystery answered, "*Bodhi* means to know one's own mind as it is."

It says in the *Avataṁsaka-sūtra:*

> Few people in the world wish to seek the *śrāvaka* vehicle. Fewer people seek the *pratyekabuddha* vehicle. Much fewer seek the Great Vehicle. It is not difficult to seek the Great Vehicle. But it is very difficult to believe in this teaching. Needless to say, it is more difficult to keep it, remember it correctly, act according to it, and understand it without error. It is not difficult to place one thousand million Sumeru worlds on one's head and remain motionless for a kalpa. But it is very difficult to believe in this teaching. Many merits will be given to anyone who offers things for pleasure for a kalpa to the living beings who are as many as the particles of dust in one thousand million Sumeru worlds. But more merits will be given to the person who believes in this teaching. It is not difficult to grasp ten Buddha worlds and stay in the sky for a kalpa. But it is very difficult to believe in this teaching. Many merits will be given to the person who offers things for pleasure for a kalpa to the living beings who are as many as the particles of dust in ten Buddha worlds. But more merits will be given to the person who believes in this teaching. Many merits will be given to the person who respectfully makes offerings for a kalpa to the Tathāgatas who are as many as the particles of dust in ten Buddha worlds. But more merits will be given for keeping this chapter.

It says in the *Mahāparinirvāṇa-sūtra:*

> Although these Mahayana Vaipulya sutras have innumerable merits, this sutra has more merits, not one hundred times more, not one thousand million times more, but beyond any calculation or explanation by similes. Good men! Milk comes from a cow. Cream comes from milk. Curdled milk comes from cream. Butter comes from curdled milk.

> Ghee comes from butter. Ghee has the best taste. Those who take ghee will eliminate all diseases because ghee includes all medicines in itself. Good men! The same can be 226a
> said of the Buddha. The *Sutra of Twelve Elements* [*Avataṁsaka-sūtra*] comes from the Buddha. The Āgama sutras come from the *Sutra of Twelve Elements*. The Vaipulya sutras come from the Āgama sutras. The *Mahāprajñāpāramitā-sūtra* comes from the Vaipulya sutras. The *Mahāparinirvāṇa-sūtra* comes from the *Mahāprajñāpāramitā-sūtra*. The *Mahāparinirvāṇa-sūtra* is like ghee. Here ghee is compared to Buddha-nature.

When compared with "the most excellent of all the sutras ever expounded, being expounded, or to be expounded" or "the sutras of six difficulties against the sutras of nine easinesses" stated in the *Saddharmapuṇḍarīka-sūtra,* the words of these sutras are as insignificant as the stars compared with the moon or as the nine mountains compared with Mount Sumeru. But even persons who seemed to have the eyes of the Buddha, such as Ch'eng-kuan of the Kegon Sect, Tz'u-en of the Hossō Sect, Chia-hsiang of the Sanron Sect, and Kōbō of the Shingon Sect, could not find this difference. Needless to say, the scholars of today, who are like blind men, cannot judge which is superior. They cannot distinguish black from white, or Mount Sumeru's size from a poppy seed's size. Needless to say, they cannot tell right from wrong in regard to the Dharma world, which is as vast as the sky. One cannot see the profundity of a teaching without knowing the status of the sutra in which the teaching is expounded.

I quoted from these sutras to help foolish people understand the difference between these sutras and the *Saddharmapuṇḍarīka-sūtra*. It would be difficult to understand this difference if I at first quoted from the sutras expounded later, and then quoted from the sutras expounded earlier.

It says in the *Daiun-kyō* that the *Daiun-kyō* is the king of sutras. We should bear in mind that there are two kinds of kings, the king of a large country and the king of a small country.

It says in the *Ghanavyūha-sūtra* that the *Ghanavyūha-sūtra* is the most excellent of all the sutras. "All" is sometimes applied to a limited number.

The simile of the five tastes of milk is applied to some part of the teachings of the Buddha, not to the whole of them, in the *Ropparamitsu-kyō*. According to the *Ropparamitsu-kyō,* those who have Buddha-nature can become Buddhas, but those who do not have Buddha-nature cannot become Buddhas. [This is different from the *Mahāparinirvāṇa-sūtra,* in which those living beings without Buddha-nature also are allowed to become Buddhas.] The simile of the five tastes of milk is applied to all the teachings of the Buddha in the *Mahāparinirvāṇa-sūtra*. Needless to say, the *Ropparamitsu-kyō* does not refer to the eternity of Śākyamuni Buddha. The eternity of Śākyamuni Buddha is expounded only in the "Discourse" [of the Original Buddha] of the *Saddharmapuṇḍarīka-sūtra,* not in the "Discourse of the Historical Buddha" in the sutra.

But Kōbō Daishi of Japan was misled by the *Ropparamitsu-kyō*. He likened the *Saddharmapuṇḍarīka-sūtra* to butter, which is the fourth of the five tastes of milk. Even the teaching of *dhāraṇī*s in the *Ropparamitsu-kyō,* which he compared to ghee, the fifth and best taste, is inferior to the *Mahāparinirvāṇa-sūtra*. I do not know why Kōbō Daishi made such a big mistake. He said, "The scholars of China competed with each other to take the taste of ghee from the *Ropparamitsu-kyō,*" treating T'ien-t'ai and his followers as thieves. Furthermore, he praised his own sect, saying, "It is regrettable that the wise men in the past did not taste ghee." I will stop discussing all this for now.

Now I will write for my followers. Other people will not believe
226b me. They will be against us.

Know whether water is seawater or not by licking a drop of it! Know whether spring has come or not by seeing a flower! You can see whether a sutra is superior or not even though you do not cross the sea of ten thousand miles to go to Sung, even though you do not spend three years to visit Mount Sacred Eagle, even though you do not enter the palace of dragons like Nāgārjuna, even though you do not see Maitreya Bodhisattva like Asaṅga Bodhisattva, even though you do not join the three sessions at the two locations of the *Saddharmapuṇḍarīka-sūtra*. Snakes foresee the coming of a flood within seven days because they are followers of dragons. Crows can tell fortunes and misfortunes throughout the year because they were fortune-tellers in their previous existences. Birds fly better than men. Nichiren knows the superiority of a sutra better than Ch'eng-kuan of the Kegon Sect, Chia-hsiang of the Sanron Sect, Tz'u-en of the Hossō Sect, and Kōbō of the Shingon Sect, because I am the follower of T'ien-t'ai and Dengyō. Unless they follow T'ien-t'ai and Dengyō, they will not be able to expiate their sin of slandering the Dharma.

I may be the richest man in Japan today. I have dedicated myself to the *Saddharmapuṇḍarīka-sūtra*. I shall be remembered forever. The god of the ocean is followed by the gods of rivers. The god of Mount Sumeru is followed by the gods of other mountains. If you understand the difference between the sutras of six difficulties and the sutras of nine easinesses expounded in the *Saddharmapuṇḍarīka-sūtra,* you will be able to understand all the sutras without reading them.

We have already seen the three testimonies quoted from the "Chapter on Beholding the Stupa of Treasures." Now I will show you two other testimonies, which are given in the "Chapter on Devadatta."

The Fourth Testimony

Devadatta was an *icchantika* but was assured of becoming Devarāja Tathāgata in the "Chapter on Devadatta." *Icchantika*s' attainment of Buddhahood is assured only verbally in the *Mahāparinirvāṇa-sūtra* compiled in forty volumes. [There is no mention of the fact that a particular *icchantika* attained Buddhahood.] *Icchantika*s' attaining Buddhahood materialized for the first time in this chapter of the *Saddharmapuṇḍarīka-sūtra*. Sunakkhatta Bhikṣu, King Ajātaśatru, and innumerable other evil persons who had committed the five sins and the sin of slandering the Dharma, were represented here in this chapter by one person, Devadatta, the gravest sinner. Here ten thousand people were represented by one person; minor sinners, by the gravest one. All the people who had committed the five sins, the seven sins, and the sin of slandering the Dharma as well as *icchantika*s were assured of Buddhahood when Devadatta was given the name of Devarāja Tathāgata. Poison changed to nectar, the most delicious drink.

The Fifth Testimony

The daughter of a dragon king became a Buddha in this chapter.
226c This does not mean that only one woman became a Buddha. It means that all women can become Buddhas. No woman is allowed to become a Buddha in the Hinayana sutras expounded before the *Saddharmapuṇḍarīka-sūtra*. It seems that some Mahayana sutras admit that women can become Buddhas or go to a Buddha world, but the Buddhahood or admittance into a Buddha world allowed to women in those sutras is only nominal because in those sutras women are required to perform the bodhisattva practices for a long time, while the teaching of one mind–three thousand assures them of [instant] attainment of Buddhahood.

A proverb says, "One represents many." The fact that the daughter of a dragon king became a Buddha paved the way for all women living in the Age of Degeneration to attain Buddhahood or enter into a Buddha world.

The filial piety of Confucian ethics is a virtue to be practiced only by those whose parents are still alive. Confucian saints and sages are such in name only because they cannot save their parents in the afterworld. Brahmans know the past and future, but they do not know how to save their parents in the future. Buddhist saints and sages deserve to be called so because they can save their parents in their future lives. But it is difficult to attain even one's own Buddhahood by following the Hinayana and Mahayana sutras expounded before the *Saddharmapuṇḍarīka-sūtra*. Needless to say, it is more difficult to have one's parents attain Buddhahood. The statement in some other sutras that anyone can attain Buddhahood is not confirmed in reality. When a woman became a Buddha in the *Saddharmapuṇḍarīka-sūtra,* a mother's attainment of Buddhahood was assured. When Devadatta, the evil man, became a Buddha, a father's attainment of Buddhahood was guaranteed. This sutra is the *Book of Filial Piety* (*Kōkyō, Hsiao-ching*) of Buddhism.

The salvation of evil men is the fourth testimony to the truthfulness of my faith; and the salvation of women, the fifth.

Astonished at these five testimonies, the bodhisattvas vowed to propagate this sutra in the "Chapter on Encouragement of Keeping the Sutra." The words of these bodhisattvas show us that the leaders of the Zen, Ritsu, and Nembutsu Sects and adherents of these sects today are slandering the Dharma.

Chapter IV

The Age of Degeneration

The Three Kinds of Arrogant People

A man called Nichiren was beheaded at the time of rat and cow at midnight on the twelfth day of the ninth month last year. What is writing this is his soul. His soul came to this country of Sado, and is now writing this for his followers. This is the second month. It is snowing. This writing appears to be dreadful, but it is not so. Some of his followers may be afraid of being persecuted when they read this. This is written according to the prophecy given by Śākyamuni, Prabhūtaratna, and the Buddhas of the worlds of the ten quarters. You should regard this as a memento of Nichiren.

The bodhisattvas say to the Buddha in the "Chapter on Encouragement of Keeping the Sutra":

> Do not worry! We will expound this sutra in the dreadful,
> evil world after your extinction. Ignorant people will speak 227a
> ill of us, abuse us, and threaten us with swords or sticks. But we will endure all this. Some *bhikṣus* in the evil world will be cunning. They will be ready to flatter others. Thinking that they have obtained what they have not, their minds will be filled with arrogance. Some *bhikṣus* will live in *araṇyas* [secluded places] and wear patched pieces of cloth. Thinking that they are practicing the true way, they will despise others. Being attached to worldly profits, they will expound the Dharma to men in white robes. They will be respected by the people of the world as arhats who have the

six supernatural powers. They will have evil thoughts. They will always think of worldly things. Even when they live in *araṇyas*, they will take pleasure in saying that we have faults.... In order to speak ill of us, in order to slander us before the great multitude, in order to say that we are evil, they will say to kings, ministers, brahmans, and also to householders and other *bhikṣus*, "They have wrong views. They are expounding heretical views."... Many dreadful things will occur in the evil world of the kalpa of defilements. Devils will enter the bodies of those *bhikṣus* and cause them to abuse and insult us.... Evil *bhikṣus* in the defiled world will not know the expedient teachings that you expounded according to the capacities of all living beings. They will speak ill of us, or frown on us, or drive us out of our monasteries from time to time.

It says in the *Hokkemongu-ki* (*Fa-Hua-wen-chü-chi*), Volume VIII:

This quotation shows the three kinds of arrogant people:

1. Arrogant laymen are referred to in the statement, "Ignorant people... but we will endure all this."

2. Arrogant *bhikṣus* are referred to in the statement, "Some *bhikṣus* in the evil world... filled with arrogance."

3. Arrogant would-be saints are referred to in the statement, "Some *bhikṣus* will live in *araṇyas*.... They are expounding the teachings of heretics."

The first kind of arrogant people may be endurable. The second kind is less endurable. The third kind is the least endurable. It is more difficult to detect the evils of the second kind than those of the first kind, and is the most difficult to detect the evils of the third kind. It is harder to detect the evils of the kind mentioned later than those of the kind mentioned earlier.

Chih-tu Fa-shih of Tung-ch'un says:

The statement, "Ignorant people... but we will endure all this," means, "Ignorant people... but we will endure the three kinds of acts of evil men except evil *bhikṣus*."

The statement, "Some *bhikṣus* in the evil world" means, "Arrogant *bhikṣus* in the evil worlds."

The statement, "Some *bhikṣus* will live in *araṇyas*... in saying that we have faults," means, "All evil men will live in *araṇyas*... in saying that we have faults."

The statement, "In order to speak ill of us.... They are expounding the teachings of heretics," means that they will approach the government and slander the Dharma and the keeper of the Dharma.

It says in the *Mahāparinirvāṇa-sūtra,* Volume IX:

Good man! Suppose an *icchantika* takes the form of an arhat, and slanders the Mahayana Vaipulya sutras in a secluded place. Ordinary men who see him will think that he is a real arhat and great bodhisattva.... This sutra will be propagated in Jambudvīpa. At that time many evil *bhikṣus* will erase the good color, smell, and taste of the right teachings of the Buddha by reshuffling the contents of this sutra, or dividing this sutra into many parts. Although they read and recite this sutra, they will eliminate the profound teachings of the Tathāgata by decorating this sutra with senseless words from the secular world, or by moving words which are placed at the beginning of this sutra to the end of this sutra, from the end to the beginning, from the beginning or the end to the middle, or from the middle to the beginning or the end. Know this! These evil *bhikṣus* are colleagues of Māra.

It says in the *Hatsunaion-gyō* (*Pan-ni-yüan-ching*), compiled 227b
in six volumes:

An *icchantika* took the form of an arhat and did evil. An arhat took the form of an *icchantika* and had compassion

> toward others. The *icchantika* in the form of an arhat slandered the Vaipulya sutras before the multitude. The arhat in the form of an *icchantika* abused *śrāvaka*s and expounded the Vaipulya sutras, saying to the people, "You and I are bodhisattvas because all living beings have the nature of the Tathāgata." But the people who heard this thought that the person who said this was an *icchantika*.

It says in the *Mahāparinirvāṇa-sūtra:*

> The Age of the Right Teachings of the Buddha will come after my extinction. The Age of the Counterfeit of the Right Teachings of the Buddha will come after the Age of the Right Teachings of the Buddha. In that age will appear a *bhikṣu* who will pretend to keep the precepts. He will read and recite sutras a little, keep his health by devouring food and drink, and wear a priestly robe. He will always say, "I have attained arhatship," as carefully as a hunter approaches game or as a cat watches a rat. He will pretend to be wise and good although he is greedy and jealous in his heart. He will be like a brahman who practices silence. He will not be a *śramaṇa* although he will look like one. He will have many wrong views and slander the right teachings of the Buddha.

The teachings of the Buddha expounded in the sutra on Mount Sacred Eagle and the sutra on the Buddha's deathbed between the two trees are as bright as the sun and the moon. The meaning of the words given by Miao-le of P'i-t'an (Bidan) and Chih-tu of Tung-ch'un is as clear as a stainless mirror. In that mirror are clearly reflected the ugly faces of the teachers of the Zen, Ritsu, and Nembutsu Sects in this country today.

It says in the *Myōhōrenge-kyō,* "in the dreadful, evil world after your extinction."

The "Chapter on Peaceful Practices" reads:

> [I]n the evil world after your extinction . . . in the Age of

> Degeneration...in the latter days after my extinction when the teachings are about to be destroyed....

The "Chapter on the Variety of Merits" says, "in the evil world in the Age of Degeneration." In the "Chapter on the Previous Life of Medicine King Bodhisattva," it says, "in the latter five hundred years after...."

The *Tembon-myōhōrenge-kyō* (*T'ien-p'in-miao-fa-lien-hua-ching*) also has the same expressions. In the "Chapter on Encouragement of Expounding the Dharma" of the *Shōhoke-kyō,* the expression "in the latter days after that" is repeated.

The Enemies of the *Saddharma-puṇḍarīka-sūtra*

T'ien-t'ai says:

> The three sects in South China and the seven sects in North China are the enemies of the *Saddharmapuṇḍarīka-sūtra* in the Age of the Counterfeit of the Right Teachings of the Buddha.

Dengyō says:

> The scholars of the sects of Nara are the enemies of the *Saddharmapuṇḍarīka-sūtra* toward the end of the Age of the Counterfeit of the Right Teachings of the Buddha.

But the enemies of the *Saddharmapuṇḍarīka-sūtra* in the times of T'ien-t'ai and Dengyō were not so conspicuous as those of today.

In the presence of the Lord Teacher Śākyamuni, the World-honored One, and Prabhūtaratna Buddha, both of whom were sitting side by side in the stupa of treasures just like the sun and the moon, and also in the presence of the Replica-Buddhas of the worlds of the ten quarters who were sitting under trees like the stars, the eighty billion *nayutas* of bodhisattvas prophesied that the three 227c
kinds of enemies of the *Saddharmapuṇḍarīka-sūtra* would appear

at the beginning of the Age of Degeneration. They said that the Age of Degeneration would come two thousand years after the extinction of the Buddha, that is to say, after one thousand years of the Age of the Right Teachings of the Buddha and one thousand years of the Age of the Counterfeit of the Right Teachings of the Buddha. Was the prophecy of those bodhisattvas false?

Now is two thousand two hundred–odd years after the extinction of the Tathāgata. It is quite easy to point to the ground with a finger. It is quite natural for a flower to bloom in spring. But even if we cannot point to the ground with our fingers, or even if a flower does not bloom in spring, it cannot be that the three kinds of enemies of the *Saddharmapuṇḍarīka-sūtra* do not exist in Japan. Who are they? Who is the practitioner of the *Saddharmapuṇḍarīka-sūtra*? I wonder. Are we among the three kinds of enemies? Or are we among the practitioners of the *Saddharmapuṇḍarīka-sūtra*? I am quite anxious about all this.

At midnight on the eighth day of the fourth month of the twenty-fourth regnal year of King Chao-wang (Shō-ō), who was the fourth king of the Chou dynasty, five-colored rays of light were emitted from the southern sky to the northern sky, making the whole sky like day. The earth quaked in the six ways. The water of rivers, wells, and ponds rose in spite of no rainfall. All the trees and grasses blossomed and bore fruits. It was very strange. The king was astonished. Prime Minister Su-yu (Soyū) divined and said, "A saint was born in the west." The king asked him, "Does his birth have any connection with our country?" Su-yu answered, "Not now. But one thousand years from now, the words of the saint will be introduced here for the benefit of the people of this country."

Su-yu was a Confucian. He had not yet eliminated any illusion caused by false judgment or evil desire, but was able to foretell an event to take place one thousand years later. As he prophesied, Buddhism was introduced into China in the tenth year of Yung-p'ing of the second Emperor Ming-ti of the Later Han dynasty.

Not comparable with the fortune-telling of this minor Confucian, the prophecy of the bodhisattvas was made in the presence of Śākyamuni, Prabhūtaratna, and the Replica-Buddhas of the worlds of the ten quarters. How can it be that the three kinds of enemies of the *Saddharmapuṇḍarīka-sūtra* are not living in Japan today? The Buddha said in the *Fuhōzō-kyō* and in other sutras that his right teachings would be propagated by twenty-four persons in succession during the Age of the Right Teachings of the Buddha, that is, one thousand years after his extinction. The twenty-four persons included Kāśyapa and Ānanda, both of whom lived in the time of the Buddha. Pārśva Bhikṣu appeared one hundred years after his extinction. Aśvaghoṣa appeared six hundred 228a
years after that. Nāgārjuna appeared seven hundred years after that. All of them appeared as had been prophesied.

The prophecy of the bodhisattvas must prove to be true. Otherwise, the whole of this sutra will lose its truthfulness. The Buddha's prophecy that Śāriputra will become Padmaprabha Tathāgata, or that Kāśyapa will become Raśmiprabhāsa Tathāgata, will become a lie. If the sutras expounded before the *Saddharmapuṇḍarīka-sūtra* become true, *śrāvaka*s will never have a chance to become Buddhas. If so, we shall be able to make offerings to dogs or foxes, but not to Ānanda and other *śrāvaka*s. This is unreasonable.

The First Kind of Enemy of the *Saddharmapuṇḍarīka-sūtra*

The first kind of enemy of the *Saddharmapuṇḍarīka-sūtra* is the first kind of arrogant people, called "ignorant people." They support the second kind of arrogant people, mentioned as "some *bhikṣu*s in the evil world," and the third kind of arrogant people, given as "some *bhikṣu*s who will live in *araṇya*s."

The first kind of arrogant people were called laymen by Miao-le Ta-shih. Chih-tu of Tung-ch'un said that they would "approach the government."

The Second Kind of Enemy of the *Saddharmapuṇḍarīka-sūtra*

The second kind of enemy of the *Saddharmapuṇḍarīka-sūtra* is "some *bhikṣus*" in the following quotation:

> Some *bhikṣus* in the evil world will be cunning. They will be ready to flatter others. Thinking that they have obtained what they have not, their minds will be filled with arrogance.

They are the "evil *bhikṣus*" in the following quotation from the *Mahāparinirvāṇa-sūtra:*

> At that time there will be evil *bhikṣus*. . . . Although they read and recite this sutra, they will eliminate the profound teachings of the Tathāgata.

It says in the *Makashikan:*

> Those who do not believe the *Saddharmapuṇḍarīka-sūtra* say, "This sutra is for saints. We are too ignorant to understand it." Those who do not have wisdom are arrogant and think that they are equal to the Buddha.

Tao-ch'o Ch'an-shih (Dōshaku Zenji) says, "Second, the way of saints is difficult to understand because the teaching is too profound for people to understand."

Hōnen says, "The practices of the way of saints are not suitable to the people of today."

It says in the *Hokkemongu-ki,* Volume X:

> It is most probable that they misunderstand this sutra because they do not know that the merits for beginners in bodhisattva practices are great. Therefore, I will now show them the power of this sutra by telling them that the beginners have great merits although they practice little.

Dengyō Daishi says:

> The Age of the Right Teachings of the Buddha already passed a long time ago. The Age of the Counterfeit of the

> Right Teachings of the Buddha is about to end. The Age of Degeneration is near at hand. Now is the time for the people to be saved by the One Vehicle expounded in the *Saddharmapuṇḍarīka-sūtra*. Why is that? It is because it says in the "Chapter on Peaceful Practices," "in the latter days... when the teachings are about to be destroyed."

Eshin says, "None of the people of Japan can be saved by any teaching other than the Perfect Mahayana Teaching."

Which is more reliable, Tao-ch'o or Dengyō, Hōnen or Eshin? The words of Tao-ch'o and Hōnen are not testified to in any sutra, while Dengyō and Eshin speak according to the *Saddharmapuṇḍarīka-sūtra*. Furthermore, Dengyō Daishi of Hieizan was the founder of the institute for initiation into monkhood to be joined by all the monks of Japan. Why do they follow Hōnen, who was possessed by Māra, and desert the leader of all monks? If Hōnen was wise, why did he not criticize these comments of Dengyō and 228b
Eshin in his *Senchaku-hongan-nembutsu-shū*? Hōnen ignored the right views of others. The second kind of enemies of the *Saddharmapuṇḍarīka-sūtra,* who are described as "some *bhikṣus* in the evil world," are Hōnen and others who observe no precepts and have wrong views.

It says in the *Mahāparinirvāṇa-sūtra,* "Kāśyapa Bodhisattva and others said that they had had wrong views before they heard this sutra."

Miao-le says, "This statement means that the teachings of Specialized Mahayana, Hinayana, and Mahayana-cum-Hinayana are wrong views."

It says in the *Makashikan:*

> "Wrong" means "evil." Therefore, know this! Only the Perfect Mahayana is good. There are two kinds of good, relative and absolute. To follow the Perfect Mahayana is the relative good. It is against the relative evil, which opposes the Perfect Mahayana. To adhere to anything is the absolute evil. The absolute good is not to adhere to the Perfect

> Mahayana. We should emancipate ourselves from evil. To adhere even to the Perfect Mahayana is evil. Needless to say, it is evil to adhere to the other teachings.

The good of Brahmanism is evil when compared with the good of the Hinayana teachings. The good of the Hinayana teachings and of the teachings of the first four of the five tastes, and of the first three of the four teachings, is evil when compared with the good of the *Saddharmapuṇḍarīka-sūtra*. Only the *Saddharmapuṇḍarīka-sūtra* is right and good. The element of Perfect Mahayana found in the sutras expounded before the *Saddharmapuṇḍarīka-sūtra* is the relative good, which is evil when compared with the absolute good. Some say that the element of Perfect Mahayana found in the earlier sutras is not Perfect Mahayana at all. If so, the element of Perfect Mahayana found in the earlier sutras is evil because it is not regarded even as the relative good. To practice the teachings of the *Avataṁsaka-sūtra* and the *Mahāprajñāpāramitā-sūtra* is evil because these sutras, although excellent, were expounded before the *Saddharmapuṇḍarīka-sūtra*. Needless to say, to practice the teachings of less excellent sutras such as the *Kammuryōju-kyō* is evil. Hōnen said that it is not necessary to read the *Saddharmapuṇḍarīka-sūtra* because the teachings of the *Saddharmapuṇḍarīka-sūtra* are included in the *Kammuryōju-kyō,* and that we should say the *nembutsu,* and give up, shut, desert, and abandon the *Saddharmapuṇḍarīka-sūtra*. Hōnen and his disciples and supporters are the slanderers of the right teachings of the Buddha, are they not? Prabhūtaratna and the Buddhas of the worlds of the ten quarters "came here... in order to have the Dharma preserved forever." Hōnen and the followers of the Nembutsu Sect of Japan say that the *Saddharmapuṇḍarīka-sūtra* will perish and the *nembutsu* will remain in the Age of Degeneration. Are they not the enemy of the "three saints": Śākyamuni, Prabhūtaratna, and the Buddhas of the worlds of the ten quarters?

The Third Kind of Enemy of the *Saddharmapuṇḍarīka-sūtra*

The third kind of enemy of the *Saddharmapuṇḍarīka-sūtra* is some *bhikṣus* who "will live in *araṇyas*." It says in the *Saddharmapuṇḍarīka-sūtra:*

> Some *bhikṣus* will live in *araṇyas* or retired places, and wear patched pieces of cloth.... They will expound the Dharma to men in white robes. They will be respected by the people of the world as arhats who have the six supernatural powers.

It says in the *Hatsunaion-gyō* compiled in six volumes:

> An *icchantika* took the form of an arhat and did evil. An arhat took the form of an *icchantika* and had compassion 228c
> toward others. The *icchantika* in the form of an arhat slandered the Vaipulya teachings before the multitude. The arhat in the form of an *icchantika* abused *śrāvakas* and expounded the Vaipulya teachings, saying to the people, "You and I are bodhisattvas because all living beings have the nature of the Tathāgata." But the people who heard this thought that the person who said this was an *icchantika*.

It says in the *Mahāparinirvāṇa-sūtra:*

> In the Age of the Counterfeit of the Right Teachings of the Buddha after my extinction, there will appear a *bhikṣu* who will pretend to keep the precepts. He will read and recite sutras a little, keep his health by devouring food and drink, and wear a priestly robe. He will always say, "I have attained arhatship," as carefully as a hunter approaches game or as a cat watches a rat. He will pretend to be wise and good although he is greedy and jealous in his heart. He will be like a brahman who practices silence. He will not be a *śramaṇa*, although he looks like one. He will have many wrong views and slander the right teachings of the Buddha.

Miao-le says, "The third kind is the least endurable. It is harder to detect the evils of the kind mentioned later than those of the kind mentioned earlier."

During the period from the time of the dream of Emperor Ming-ti of the Later Han dynasty to the time of the Ch'en dynasty, a person transmitted the Dharma from the Buddha and introduced Zen to China.

It says in the *Hokke-sandaibu-fuchū* (*Fa-hua-san-ta-pu-pu-chu*), "'The person who transmitted the Dharma from the Buddha' means Bodhidharma."

It says in the *Makashikan,* Volume V, "Some Zen teachers and their followers are either blind because they have no wisdom or lame because they have no practice. They will fall into hell."

229a It says in the *Makashikan,* Volume VII:

> Tendai priests are required to perform ten practices. One of the ten practices is translation. They are not good at translation, but their nine other practices are satisfactory. They are different from the priests who know only letters or the Zen teachers who only practice. Some Zen teachers do nothing but introspection into their minds, and their mind introspection is not deep or true. They do none of the nine other practices. What I say is not false. Those who have eyes should know all this.

It says in the *Shikan-guketsu,* Volume VII:

> "The priests who know only letters" are the priests who read books but do not introspect their minds. "The Zen teachers who only practice" are those who care for their noses and chests but do not study the theory of consciousness.... Their meditation does not eliminate fundamental illusions. The expression: "Some Zen teachers do nothing but introspection into their minds" is not adequate. Strictly speaking, they practice neither textual study nor introspection of mind. The Zen priests of today only play with words. They do not

> memorize sutras. They form their own opinions and ignore sutras. They say that the number sixteen, which indicates the height of a statue of the Buddha, combines the number eight of the eight wrongdoings against the Eightfold Path and the number eight of the eight things to arouse our attention, or that the number eight of the eight wrongdoings against the Eightfold Path combines the number five of the five aggregates and the number three of the three poisons, or that the number six of the six sense organs means the number six of the six supernatural powers, or that the number four of the four elements means the number four of the Four Noble Truths. Such capricious interpretations of words are neither deep nor shallow, but deceptive and misleading.

It says in the *Makashikan,* Volume VII:

> A Zen Master of Yeh-lo (Gyōraku) was famous throughout China. While he stayed there, many people came to see him. When he left there, many people followed him. He was very famous, but for what profit? His followers regretted on their deathbeds that they had followed him.

It says in the *Shikan-guketsu,* Volume VII:

> Yeh is in Hsiang-chou (Sōshū) Province. It was the capital city of Chi'i and Wei (Gi). Buddhism flourished there. Bodhidharma founded the Zen Sect there and propagated it throughout the district. T'ien-t'ai did not mention Bodhidharma by name, thinking that mentioning him would trouble his followers. Lo is the present Lo-yang.

It says in the *Hatsunaion-gyō* compiled in six volumes, "It says that it is difficult to see 'the final thing.' It means that it is difficult to see the worst karmas of *icchantika*s."

Miao-le says, "The third kind is the least endurable. It is harder to detect the evils of the kind mentioned later."

Blind men, one-eyed men, or men of wrong views cannot see the three kinds of enemies of the *Saddharmapuṇḍarīka-sūtra* who appear at the beginning of the Age of Degeneration. Only those who have part of the eyes of the Buddha will be able to see them.

It says in the *Saddharmapuṇḍarīka-sūtra,* "they will say to kings, ministers, and brahmans, and also to householders. . . ."

Chih-tu Fa-shih of Tung-ch'un says, "They will approach the government and slander the Dharma and the keeper of the Dharma before the government."

Toward the end of the Age of the Counterfeit of the Right Teachings of the Buddha, Gomyō, Shuen, and others submitted their appeal to the government and slandered Dengyō Daishi. Now at the beginning of the Age of Degeneration, Ryōkan, Nen-a, and others have submitted their appeals full of falsehood to the shogun. Are they not the third kind of enemy of the *Saddharmapuṇḍarīka-sūtra*?

The followers of the Nembutsu Sect of today say to the "kings, ministers, and brahmans, and also to householders" who support the Tendai Hokke Sect, that the *Saddharmapuṇḍarīka-sūtra* is
229b "too profound for us to understand," and that its teaching is deep while the hearers are shallow-brained. Are they not the people who do not believe the *Saddharmapuṇḍarīka-sūtra,* saying, "This sutra is for saints. We are too ignorant to understand it"?

The teachers of the Zen Sect say:

> The *Saddharmapuṇḍarīka-sūtra* is the finger pointing to the moon. Zen is the moon. After you see the moon, a finger is unnecessary. Zen is the mind of the Buddha. The *Saddharmapuṇḍarīka-sūtra* is the words of the Buddha. After he expounded the *Saddharmapuṇḍarīka-sūtra* and all the other sutras, the Buddha gave a flower to Kāśyapa, and transmitted the Dharma to him. The Dharma was transmitted successively to the twenty-eighth patriarch, Bodhidharma, and then to the sixth Chinese Zen Patriarch [Hui-neng].

This false statement has already been deceiving the people of this country for a long time.

The high priests of the Tendai and Shingon Sects today are not well versed in the teachings of their own sects although they are famous in the circles of their own sects. They are greedy. They are afraid of nobles and samurai, and not only admit but also praise the teachings of the Nembutsu and Zen Sects. Prabhūtaratna and the Replica-Buddhas proved the truthfulness of the *Saddharmapuṇḍarīka-sūtra* "in order to have the Dharma preserved forever." Now the high priests of the Tendai Sect side with the Nembutsu and Zen Sects, saying, "The *Saddharmapuṇḍarīka-sūtra* is too profound for us to understand." Therefore, the *Saddharmapuṇḍarīka-sūtra* exists only in name in Japan today. No one practices this sutra to attain enlightenment.

Who is to be called the practitioner of the *Saddharmapuṇḍarīka-sūtra*? Countless monks were exiled because they burned down temples and towers. Many high priests were hated by the commoners because they flattered nobles and samurai. Are these priests to be called the practitioners of the *Saddharmapuṇḍarīka-sūtra*? The words of the Buddha are not false; therefore, the three kinds of enemies of the *Saddharmapuṇḍarīka-sūtra* are now found everywhere in this country. But, as if to disprove the truthfulness of the words of the Buddha, there is no sign appearing of the practitioner of the *Saddharmapuṇḍarīka-sūtra*. Why is that?

Who was spoken ill of and abused by laymen? What priest was threatened with swords and sticks? What priest was reported to nobles and samurai because of practicing the *Saddharmapuṇḍarīka-sūtra*? What priest was driven out of his monastery
"from time to time"? There is no such priest except me, Nichiren. 229c
But I am not the practitioner of the *Saddharmapuṇḍarīka-sūtra* because no god protects me. Whom shall we call the practitioner of the *Saddharmapuṇḍarīka-sūtra* in order to verify the words of the Buddha?

The Buddha lived with Devadatta just as a man lives with his shadow. Crown Prince Shōtoku lived with Moriya just as the flower of a lotus grows with its fruit at the same time. In the same manner, the practitioner of the *Saddharmapuṇḍarīka-sūtra* must live with the three kinds of enemies of the sutra. The three kinds of enemies have already appeared. Who is the practitioner of the *Saddharmapuṇḍarīka-sūtra*? If there is any, I will respect him as my teacher. It will be very difficult to find him, just as it is difficult for a one-eyed turtle to find a hole in a floating piece of wood.

Chapter V

Die a Martyr for the Cause of the *Saddharmapuṇḍarīka-sūtra*!

The Three Great Vows

Question: It seems that the three kinds of enemies of the *Saddharmapuṇḍarīka-sūtra* exist today. But there is no practitioner of the *Saddharmapuṇḍarīka-sūtra*. I cannot say that you are the practitioner of the *Saddharmapuṇḍarīka-sūtra* because this sutra states in many places that the practitioner of the *Saddharmapuṇḍarīka-sūtra* will be peaceful.

It says in this sutra:

> Celestial pages will serve him (anyone who reads this sutra). He will not be struck with swords or sticks. He will not be poisoned.... If anyone speaks ill of him, the speaker's mouth will be shut.... [Those who hear the Dharma] will be peaceful in their present lives. In their future lives, they will be reborn in good places.... Anyone who troubles the expounder of the Dharma shall have his head split into seven pieces just like the branches of the *arjaka* trees.... He [the keeper of this sutra] will be able to obtain the reward of his merits in his present life.... Those who, upon seeing the keeper of this sutra, blame him justly or unjustly, will suffer from white leprosy in their present lives.

Answer: I understand what you say. Let me clear up your doubts. It says in the "Chapter on Never Despising Bodhisattva,"

"Some of the four kinds of devotees spoke ill of him . . . struck him with a stick, a piece of wood, a piece of tile or a stone."

It says in the *Mahāparinirvāṇa-sūtra,* "[Those who became *bhikṣus* in order to get food] killed or hurt pure *bhikṣus*."

The Buddha says in the *Saddharmapuṇḍarīka-sūtra,* "Many people hate this sutra with jealousy even in my lifetime."

One of the toes of the Buddha bled due to the attack of Devadatta. He had nine such incidents altogether. Was the Buddha not the practitioner of the *Saddharmapuṇḍarīka-sūtra*? Can we not say that Never Despising Bodhisattva was the practitioner of the teaching of the One Vehicle? Maudgalyāyana was killed by Daṇḍapāṇi after he was assured of his attainment of Buddhahood. Deva Bodhisattva, the fourteenth patriarch, and the Venerable Siṁha, the twenty-fifth patriarch, were also killed. Were they not the practitioners of the *Saddharmapuṇḍarīka-sūtra*? Chu-tao-sheng (Jiksu Dōshō) was exiled to Su-shan (Sozan). Fa-tao (Hōdō)
230a was branded on the face and sent to Chiang-nan (Kōnan). Were they not the keepers of the teaching of the One Vehicle? Tenjin of Kitano (Sugawara-no-Michizane) and Pai-chü-i (Hakukyoi) were also exiled. Were they not sages?

I think that a person who did not commit the sin of slandering the *Saddharmapuṇḍarīka-sūtra* in his previous existence can practice the sutra in his present life. Those who persecute the practitioner of the *Saddharmapuṇḍarīka-sūtra* on the charge of a petty offense in the secular world, even though he is innocent, will be punished just as *asura*s who shot arrows at Śakra were punished at once, or as *garuḍa*s who entered the Anavatapta Pond to eat the dragon king were killed instantly.

T'ien-t'ai says, "My present suffering was caused in the past. My good deeds in my present life will be rewarded in my future life."

It says in the *Shinjikan-gyō* (*Hsin-ti-kuan-ching*), "If you want to know the cause in the past, see the effect in the present. If you want to know the effect in the future, see the cause in the present."

It says in the "Chapter on Never Despising Bodhisattva," "Thus he expiated his sin." It seems that Never Despising Bodhisattva was struck with pieces of tile or stones because he had slandered the *Saddharmapuṇḍarīka-sūtra* in his previous existence.

The person who is destined to fall into hell in his next life is not punished in the present even when he commits serious sins because he is an *icchantika*. It says in the *Mahāparinirvāṇa-sūtra:*

> Kāśyapa Bodhisattva said to the Buddha, "World-honored One! You say that the light of Great Nirvana enters the bodies of all living beings through their pores.... Some people have not yet aspired to *bodhi*. How can they obtain the cause of *bodhi?*"
>
> The Buddha said to Kāśyapa, "Suppose someone hears this *Mahāparinirvāṇa-sūtra* and slanders my right teachings, saying that he does not need to aspire to *bodhi*. He will have a dream that night. In his dream, he will be surprised to see a *rākṣasa*. The *rākṣasa* will say to him, 'Alas, good man! If you do not aspire to *bodhi* right now, I will kill you.' Frightened at hearing this, he will aspire to *bodhi*. You should know that he will become a great bodhisattva."

As long as he is not terribly evil, he will dream of a *rākṣasa* when he slanders the right teachings of the Buddha, and will aspire to *bodhi*. But an *icchantika* cannot have this dream, just as "a dead tree or a stone mountain" cannot hold rainwater, as a "scorched seed" cannot bring forth a bud "even after a gentle rain," as "the most brilliant gem cannot clear muddy water," as "a hand grasp- 230b
ing poison cannot refrain from being poisoned when it has a scar," or as "the heaviest rain cannot stay in the sky." There are many other similes. In a word, the worst *icchantika* is not punished in the present because it is certain that he will fall into the Hell of Incessant Suffering in his next life. King Chieh of the Hsia dynasty and King Chou of the Yin dynasty committed serious crimes, but there were no calamities in their countries because the downfall of their dynasties was already predestined.

I think that the worst person is not punished in the present also because the guardian gods have left this country. The guardian gods do not protect but leave a country where the people slander the Dharma. Therefore, the worst person is not punished while the practitioner of the right teachings of the Buddha is put under great difficulties. It says in the *Suvarṇaprabhāsa-sūtra,* "Those who do good karmas are decreasing in number day after day." The same can be said of Japan today. The country is not good. The time is not good, either. I dealt with all this in my *Risshō-ankoku-ron.*

After all this, I should say, "Let the gods leave our country! Let any difficulty come to me!" I will stop practicing the *Saddharma-puṇḍarīka-sūtra* only when my life expires. Śāriputra retired from his bodhisattva practices, which he had performed for sixty kalpas, because he could not bear the insult of the eye-begging brahman. Many people today have not yet been saved because they have abandoned the *Saddharmapuṇḍarīka-sūtra* at the instigation of their evil friends although they were given the seeds of Buddhahood by Mahābhijñājñānābhibhū Buddha three thousand great thousand worlds dust particles kalpas ago, and also by Śākyamuni Buddha five hundred thousand billion *nayuta asamkhya* worlds dust particles kalpas ago. For whatever reason, good or bad, to abandon the *Saddharmapuṇḍarīka-sūtra* is to go to hell. I will make great vows. Even if I am told, "The throne of Japan will be yours if you say the *nembutsu.* Abandon the *Saddharma-puṇḍarīka-sūtra,* and put your hopes for your next life in practicing the *Kammuryōju-kyō* and other sutras! If you do not say the *nembutsu,* your parents will be beheaded," I will resist all these threats unless my faith is refuted by a wise man. All the other persecutions will be just a particle of dust before the wind. I will be the pillar of Japan. I will be the eyes of Japan. I will be the great vessel of Japan. I will not break these vows.

The Expiation of My Sins

Question: Why do you say that your exiles and other persecutions are the effects of your deeds in your previous existence?

Answer: A mirror made of copper reflects everything in itself. The king of the Ch'in dynasty had a mirror that could detect any falsehood by his subjects. All the crimes of his attendants were reflected in that mirror. The mirror of the teachings of the Buddha manifests the deeds in the past. It says in the *Hatsunaion-gyō:* 230c

> Good men! The person who committed innumerable crimes and did various evil karmas in his previous existence will have his retribution in his present life. He will be despised by others. His appearance will be ugly. He will be short of clothing. His food and drink will be scanty. He will not be able to get profits although he seeks fortune. He will be born poor and to a family with wrong views. He will be persecuted by the government. He will also suffer in many other ways. He will receive these retributions in his present life. But his retributions will be less than the retributions he will receive if he does not protect the Dharma.

This statement of the sutra exactly describes what I am now. All my doubts are cleared up. All questions have become groundless. Let me read this statement word by word and think of myself. Now I will comment on it.

"He will be despised by others." It says in the *Saddharma-puṇḍarīka-sūtra,* "They will hate him, and look at him with jealousy." I have been despised by others for the past twenty-odd years.

"His appearance will be ugly. He will be short of clothing." This exactly fits me.

"His food and drink will be scanty." This refers to me.

"He will not be able to get profits although he seeks fortune." This fits me.

"He will be born poor." This expresses what I was.

"He will be persecuted by the government." How can I doubt this statement? It says in the *Saddharmapuṇḍarīka-sūtra* [that others will] "drive us out of our monasteries from time to time."

[He will also suffer] "in many other ways.... But his retributions will be less than the retributions he will receive if he does not protect the Dharma." Because I protect the Dharma, I shall be punished less, although I did evil karmas in my previous existence. As long as I protect the Dharma, I shall finally be able to cut off the bonds of birth and death.

It says in the *Makashikan,* Volume V:

> There are two kinds of good, the good of ordinary men and the good from meditation. The good of ordinary men is too weak to eliminate the effects of evil karmas in the past. Practice the *shikan* and meditate on the health and illness of your minds, and you will be able to cut off the cycle of birth and death.... [When you pursue the Right Way,] the three obstacles [passions, karma, and karmic results,] and the four devils [defilements, the five *skandha*s causing suffering, death, and *māra*] will occur, competing with one another, to disturb us.

I think I was born as an evil king and plundered food, clothing, land, and so forth from practitioners of the *Saddharmapuṇḍarīka-sūtra* countless times during my previous consecutive existences since the beginningless past, just as the people of Japan today are destroying the temples of the *Saddharmapuṇḍarīka-sūtra*. I also think that I beheaded practitioners of the *Saddharmapuṇḍarīka-sūtra* countless times during my previous consecutive existences.

I may have already expiated some of these serious sins. But even the sins that I think I have already expiated may not have been expiated satisfactorily. In order to eliminate the bonds of birth and death, I must completely expiate all the sins I have committed.

My merits are trifling while my sins are serious. When I practiced Provisional Mahayana sutras, I did not have to commit these serious sins. When you forge a sword, the scar of the sword is not visible until the iron is red enough for forging and hammering is repeated. When you press sesame seeds with more power, you get more oil from them. 231a

Now I am vehemently criticizing the slanderers of the Dharma in this country. I am persecuted probably because my protection of the Dharma has caused me to expiate the great sins that I had committed in my previous existences. Iron is black without fire, and red in fire. When a stream is checked abruptly by logs, mountainous waves will be made. When disturbed, a sleeping lion will roar.

It says in the *Mahāparinirvāṇa-sūtra:*

> A poverty-stricken woman was pregnant. She had no house, no protectors. She was ill in health, hungry, and thirsty. She wandered about, begging food. She stayed at an inn, and gave birth to a boy. The master of the inn drove away the mother and her son. Before long, after the birth, the mother left for another country, carrying her baby in her arms. On the way, they met a heavy storm. It was terribly cold. Furthermore, they were attacked by many mosquitoes, horseflies, bees, and other vermin. She crossed the Ganges River with her baby in her arms. The current was very rapid. She held her baby fast, but both mother and son were drowned. She was reborn in the Brahma Heaven because she was so compassionate toward her baby.
>
> Mañjuśrī! If a good man wishes to protect the right teachings of the Buddha, he should act like the poor woman, who died in the Ganges River because of her love for her baby. Good man! Like her, the bodhisattva who protects the Dharma should not spare his life. Then he will be able to be emancipated automatically even though he does not seek it, just as the poor woman reached the Brahma Heaven even though she did not seek to go there.

Chang-an Ta-shih (Shōan Daishi) commented on this statement with the theory of three obstacles. Observe his interpretation.

"Poverty-stricken" means "not yet having received the teachings of the Buddha." "Woman" means "a person who has a small amount of compassion." "Inn" means "a defiled world." "Boy" means the seed of Buddhahood obtained by faith in the *Saddharma-puṇḍarīka-sūtra*. "To drive away" means "to exile." "Before long after birth" means "before long after a person embraces the faith." "A heavy storm" means a sentence of banishment. "Attacked by vermin" means "spoken ill of and abused by ignorant people." "Both mother and son were drowned" means "the person who did not give up his faith in the *Saddharmapuṇḍarīka-sūtra* was beheaded." "Brahma Heaven" should be read as "the [Pure] World of the Buddha."

The truth that karma causes rebirth in another world can be applied to any of the ten regions, from hell up to the world of the Buddha. One who kills people in any country, including Japan and China, will suffer for many years in the evil regions except in
231b the Hell of Incessant Suffering, unless he commits the five sins and the sin of slandering the Dharma.

One cannot be reborn in the realm of form and become a Brahma if he practices only the good of ordinary men, even though the good of ordinary men requires observing innumerable precepts and practicing innumerable good deeds.

In order to become a Brahma, one should practice at least the first state of meditation, that is, the meditation still accompanied by illusions, and in addition should accumulate merits of compassion. The poor woman did not practice any meditation, but was reborn in the Brahma Heaven because she thought of her son. This did not accord with that requirement. Chang-an interpreted this irregularity in two ways. Judging from Chang-an's view, I think I can say the following. The mind of the mother was entirely occupied by her love for her son. The concentration of mind on this occasion resembles meditation. To think solely of her son is akin to the compassion of the Buddha. Therefore, she was reborn in the Brahma Heaven although she did nothing else.

The way to attain Buddhahood is explained variously by various sects. The Kegon Sect holds that it is by seeing the truth that the mind is all. The Sanron Sect says that it is by seeing the truth that the eight negations are the Middle Way. The Hossō Sect contends that it is by realizing the truth that what is, is only consciousness. The Shingon Sect declares that it is by realizing the truth that everything is composed of the five elements. It does not seem, however, that any of these views expresses the reality of all things.

Only the teaching of one mind–three thousand of the Tendai Sect is the way to Buddhahood. I do not have even a bit of wisdom to understand this teaching, but I am convinced that only one sutra, only the *Saddharmapuṇḍarīka-sūtra,* contains the gem of one mind–three thousand in itself. The teachings of the other sutras are just yellow stones that look like gems. You cannot get oil by pressing grains of sand. A sterile woman cannot have a child. Even wise men cannot become Buddhas by means of the other sutras. Even ignorant people can plant the seeds of Buddhahood by means of this sutra. Ignorant people will be able to become Buddhas automatically, just as the person who protects the Dharma will be able "to be emancipated even though he does not seek it."

I said to my disciples day and night:

> We shall be able to reach the world of the Buddha automatically if we have no doubts even when we have difficulties. Have no doubt that the gods will not protect us! Do not lament that we are not peaceful!

But many of them doubted me and left me. Ordinary people are apt to forget what they promised when their promises were needed. I think that they do not like to part from their wives and children, whom they love. However, during the past innumerable kalpas in their previous consecutive existences, they parted from their wives and children repeatedly. Did they part from them peacefully? Did they part from them for the cause of the teachings of the 231c
Buddha? They must have parted from them in tears in any case.

Go to the Pure World of Mount Sacred Eagle without giving up your faith in the *Saddharmapuṇḍarīka-sūtra,* and lead your wives and children there!

Submissive and Aggressive

Question: You say that the followers of the Nembutsu and Zen Sects will be sent to the Hell of Incessant Suffering. You are aggressive. You will fall into the region of *asuras*. It says in the "Chapter on Peaceful Practices" in the *Saddharmapuṇḍarīka-sūtra,* "You should not point out the faults of other persons or sutras. You should not despise other teachers of the Dharma." I think that you are deserted by the gods because you go against this warning of the Buddha.

Answer: It says in the *Makashikan:*

> There are two ways of propagating the Dharma, the submissive way and the aggressive way. It says in the "Chapter on Peaceful Practices," "You should not speak of the good points or bad points...." This is the submissive way. The *Mahāparinirvāṇa-sūtra* reads, "You should carry a sword or a stick... behead him." This is the aggressive way. Although different from each other, both ways benefit all living beings.

It says in the *Shikan-guketsu:*

> It says in the *Makashikan,* "There are two ways...." The *Mahāparinirvāṇa-sūtra* reads, "You should carry a sword or a stick...." The *Mahāparinirvāṇa-sūtra,* Volume III, says, "The person who protects the right teachings of the Buddha will be able to be reborn in the World of Akṣobhya even though he does not keep the five precepts or practice proper deportments.... King Seer Prophet beheaded the slanderers of the Dharma.... The king prohibited the use of older medicine, which was found to be poisonous, and ordered that those who used the older medicine should be

> beheaded. . . ." All this shows the aggressive way of eliminating the destroyers of the Dharma. In any sutra or *śāstra*, we cannot find any other way of propagating the Dharma than these two.

It says in the *Hokkemongu-ki:*

> Question: It says in the *Mahāparinirvāṇa-sūtra,* "Approach the king, take up swords and arrows, and defeat evil persons!" But it says in the *Saddharmapuṇḍarīka-sūtra* that we should not approach kings and nobles, and that we should be humble, modest, and compassionate toward others. The former is hard while the latter is soft. How can we say that the two ways are the same in benefiting all living beings?
>
> Answer: The *Mahāparinirvāṇa-sūtra* deals with the aggressive way, but it also says that all living beings are like Rāhula, the only son of the Buddha. This indicates that the *Mahāparinirvāṇa-sūtra* also has the submissive way of propagating the Dharma. The *Saddharmapuṇḍarīka-sūtra* emphasizes the submissive way, but it also says, "Anyone who . . . troubles the expounder of the Dharma shall have his head split into seven pieces." This shows that the *Saddharmapuṇḍarīka-sūtra* also has the aggressive way. Each of the two sutras emphasizes one or the other way of propagating the Dharma to meet the needs of the time.

It says in the *Nehangyō-sho* (*Nieh-p'an-ching-su*):

> It says in the *Mahāparinirvāṇa-sūtra* that any monk or layman who wishes to protect the Dharma should propagate the great teaching by keeping his original intention, that is, by forsaking formalism and preserving fundamental principles. By doing so, he can "protect the right teachings of the Buddha." He should not be attached to trivial matters. Therefore, he does "not practice proper deportments." In the olden days the Dharma was propagated peacefully, and the monks had only to observe the precepts. They did not have to carry sticks. But now the world is not peaceful, and

> the Dharma is ignored. Therefore, monks should carry sticks. They should not observe the precepts. When the world is not peaceful, they should carry sticks. When the world is peaceful, they should observe the precepts. They should choose one according to the needs of the time. They should not constantly cling to either of the two.

The scholars of today will think that your doubts are quite reasonable. Even my disciples think so because they are like
232a *icchantika*s. Therefore, I quoted from the writings of T'ien-t'ai and Miao-le to clear up their doubts.

The submissive way is as different from the aggressive way as water is from fire. Fire dislikes water. Water hates fire. Submissive men laugh at aggressive men. Aggressive men feel sorry for submissive men. When a country is filled with ignorant and evil people, the submissive way should be used first, as is shown in the "Chapter on Peaceful Practices." When many people have wrong views and slander the Dharma, the aggressive way should be applied first, as is given in the "Chapter on Never Despising Bodhisattva." When the weather is hot, we use cold water. When it is cold, we like fire. Plants are followers of the sun. They suffer under the winter moon. Waters are followers of the moon. When it is hot, they lose their natural coldness.

In the Age of Degeneration, both ways are necessary because there are two kinds of countries, evil countries where many people are ignorant and evil, and Dharma-destroying countries where many people have wrong views and slander the Dharma. You should know whether present-day Japan is an evil country or a Dharma-destroying country.

Question: Is it efficient to practice the aggressive way when the submissive way is needed, or to practice the submissive way when the aggressive way is needed?

Answer: It says in the *Mahāparinirvāṇa-sūtra:*

> Kāśyapa Bodhisattva said to the Buddha, "World-honored One! I know that the *dharmakāya* of the Tathāgata is

> indestructible like a diamond. I do not know why. Please explain it!"
>
> The Buddha said, "Kāśyapa! I was able to obtain this diamond-like body because I protected the right Dharma. Kāśyapa! I was able to obtain this eternally indestructible diamond-like body because I protected the Dharma in the past. Good man! Those who protect the right teachings of the Buddha do not have to keep the five precepts, or practice proper deportments, but have to carry swords, bows, arrows, and halberds. . . ." The *bhikṣus* who keep the five precepts will expound the Dharma, but they will not be able to make a lion's roar, defeat unjust and evil men, or benefit themselves or others. Know this! They are idle and lazy. Although they keep the precepts and protect pure deeds, know this, they will not be able to do anything else. . . . Suppose a teacher of the Dharma does not keep the precepts but makes a lion's roar and criticizes unjust *bhikṣus*. Hearing his criticism, those *bhikṣus* will get angry and kill the teacher of the Dharma. Even if he is dead, he should be considered to be keeping the precepts, and benefiting himself and others.

Chang-an says, "They should choose one according to the needs of the time. They should not constantly cling to either of the two." T'ien-t'ai says, "to meet the needs of the time." It is difficult to 232b
harvest a crop of rice if we sow the seeds and till the soil at the end of autumn.

Hōnen and Dainichi appeared in the years of Kennin, and propagated the Nembutsu and Zen Sects. Hōnen said, "In the Age of Degeneration, no one has attained Buddhahood by the *Saddharmapuṇḍarīka-sūtra* . . . not one among a thousand people." Dainichi said, "Zen was transmitted from the Buddha to us without sutras."

These two sects are now popular all over this country. The scholars of the Tendai and Shingon Sects flatter the supporters of the Nembutsu and Zen Sects just as a dog wags its tail before its master, or fear them just as a rat shudders before a cat. They obtain positions in the government and tell emperors and shoguns their views, which will eventually destroy Buddhism and this country. They are now like hungry spirits. They will be sent to the Hell of Incessant Suffering in their future lives. Even if they sit in mountains and forests and meditate on the teaching of one mind–three thousand, or even if they sit in secluded places and keep unspilled the water of the three mystic things, they will not be able to get rid of birth and death because they do not know the needs of the time and the difference between the submissive way and the aggressive way.

Question: What profit can we expect when we criticize the people of the Nembutsu and Zen Sects and are hated by them?

Answer: It says in the *Mahāparinirvāṇa-sūtra:*

> Suppose a good *bhikṣu,* upon seeing people who destroy the Dharma, does not reproach them, drive them away, or punish them. Know this! He is an enemy of the teachings of the Buddha. If he drives them away, reproaches, or punishes them, he is my disciple, my hearer in the true sense of the word.

Chang-an says:

> Those who destroy the teachings of the Buddha are enemies of the teachings of the Buddha. The person who pretends to be their friend is their enemy. He has no compassion toward them. If he criticizes them, he is a Dharma-protecting hearer, who is to be called my true disciple. He will be their true friend when he removes their evils. He will be my true disciple when he reproaches them. If he does not drive them away, he will become an enemy of the teachings of the Buddha.

In the "Chapter on Beholding the Stupa of Treasures" in the *Saddharmapuṇḍarīka-sūtra,* Śākyamuni, Prabhūtaratna, and all the Replica-Buddhas of the worlds of the ten quarters assembled in this Sahā world. For what purpose? I think that those Buddhas assembled for the purpose of giving the *Saddharmapuṇḍarīka-sūtra* to all the sons of the Buddha in the future. It seems that their compassion toward all living beings is greater than the com- 232c passion of parents toward their only son who is suffering much. But Hōnen did not think of the minds of those Buddhas, and shut the gate to the *Saddharmapuṇḍarīka-sūtra* against the people, saying that the *Saddharmapuṇḍarīka-sūtra* is useless in the Age of Degeneration. He had the people abandon the *Saddharmapuṇḍarīka-sūtra*, just as a poor and evil man had the perverted son of a rich man throw away his treasures by deceiving the son. Hōnen was merciless, indeed.

Do you not tell your parents when you realize that someone is attempting to kill them? Do you not stop a drunken son from killing his parents? Do you not keep an evil man from setting fire to temples and towers? Do you not treat your son with moxa when he is seriously ill? Those who do not admonish the followers of the Zen and Nembutsu Sects of Japan are like those who do nothing on these occasions. Chang-an says, "The person who pretends to be their friend is their enemy. He has no compassion toward them."

I am the dear parent of all the people of Japan. All the people of the Tendai Sect today are their great enemies. Chang-an says, "He will be their true friend when he removes their evils." They have no aspiration for enlightenment. They cannot get rid of birth and death.

The Lord Teacher Śākyamuni, the World-honored One, was abused as the most vicious man by all brahmans. T'ien-t'ai Tashih was spoken ill of by the three sects in South China and the seven sects in North China, and was criticized by Tokuichi, who said, "The five-foot body of T'ien-t'ai was mutilated by the three-inch tongue." Dengyō Daishi was reproached by the priests of [the sects of] Nara, who said, "Saichō has not yet visited the capital city of T'ang." Śākyamuni, T'ien-t'ai, and Dengyō were treated so badly. It was not a shame, however, because they suffered for the cause of the *Saddharmapuṇḍarīka-sūtra*. It is the greatest shame to be praised by ignorant people. The priests of the Tendai and

Shingon Sects will be glad to see me persecuted. They are pitiful and shameful.

Śākyamuni, the World-honored One, entered the defiled world called Sahā. Kumārajīva traveled all the way to Ch'in. Dengyō visited China with great difficulties. Deva and Siṁha were killed. Bhaiṣajyarāja burned his arms [to make an offering of light to the Buddha]. Crown Prince Shōtoku peeled the skin on his hand and put it on the cover of a copy of a sutra. Śākyamuni sold his flesh when he was a bodhisattva in his previous existence. Delight Dharma Bodhisattva wrote a *gāthā* using his bone as a writing brush. T'ien-t'ai says, "to meet the needs of the time." The practice of the teachings of the Buddha is different according to the
233a needs of the time.

My exile is not lamentable because it is minor suffering in my present life. My exile is great pleasure because I shall thereby be able to have great happiness in my next life.

Glossary

arhat ("worthy one"): A saint who has completely eradicated all passions and attained emancipation from the cycles of birth and death; the highest state of spiritual attainment in the Hinayana. *See also* Hinayana.

asura: A class of demonic beings who are in constant conflict with the gods.

bodhi: Enlightenment; a state in which one is awakened to the true nature of things.

bodhisattva: In the Mahayana, a passionless, selfless being with universal compassion who is destined to become a Buddha but who delays his or her entry into Buddhahood in order to help liberate all sentient beings. *See also* Mahayana; three vehicles.

dhāraṇī: A mystical phrase, spell, or incantation.

Eightfold Path: The path by which suffering can be ended, consisting of: (1) right view, (2) right thought, (3) right speech, (4) right action, (5) right livelihood, (6) right effort, (7) right mindfulness, and (8) right meditation.

five sins: (1) Patricide, (2) matricide, (3) killing an arhat, (4) maliciously harming a Buddha, and (5) causing disharmony in the Buddhist order.

five precepts: (1) Not to kill, (2) not to steal, (3) not to commit adultery, (4) not to lie, and (5) not to drink intoxicants.

five *skandhas:* The five aggregates that make up sentient beings—(1) form (*rūpa*), (2) sensation (*vedanā*), (3) conception (*saṃjñā*), (4) volition (*saṃskāra*), and (5) consciousness (*vijñāna*).

Four Noble Truths: (1) Life is intrinsically full of suffering; (2) attachment is the cause of suffering; (3) all suffering can be ended; (4) the way to end suffering is by following the Buddha's Eightfold Path. *See also* Eightfold Path.

garuḍa: A mythological giant bird.

gāthā: A verse of Buddhist scripture or teachings, a Buddhist hymn.

Hinayana ("Lesser Vehicle"): A derogatory term applied by Mahayana Buddhists to the various schools of early Buddhism that exalt as their ideal the arhat. *See also* Mahayana.

icchantika: A person who does not have roots of merit and therefore can never become a Buddha by his or her own power.

kalpa: An immense period of time, an eon.

Mahayana ("Great Vehicle"): A form of Buddhism that appeared in India around 100 B.C.E. and that exalts as its religious ideal the bodhisattva. *See also* bodhisattva.

māra: A kind of demon that hinders Buddhist practice.

Middle Way: The truth of nonduality taught by Śākyamuni Buddha.

One Vehicle: The teaching of the *Lotus Sutra* that all beings are destined for the single goal of Buddhahood, and that there is only one vehicle, not three vehicles, through which to attain enlightenment. *See also* three vehicles.

pratyekabuddha ("solitary enlightened one"): One who has attained enlightenment through his or her own power. A *pratyekabuddha* had no teacher, does not teach, and lacks universal compassion. *See also* three vehicles.

samādhi: A mental state of concentration involving the focusing of thought on one object. Also called meditation.

śāstra: A Buddhist treatise, a scholastic work, sometimes a commentary on a sutra.

śrāvaka ("word-hearer"): Originally, a disciple of Śākyamuni, one who heard his teachings; later used as a general term for so-called Hinayana Buddhists. *See also* Hinayana; three vehicles.

stupa: A reliquary, a roughly hemispherical structure enshrining the relics of the Buddha or some other Buddhist teacher, or copies of Buddhist scriptures.

sutra: A discourse of the Buddha.

three evil regions: The three realms into which sentient beings transmigrate as retribution for evil deeds—(1) hell, (2) the realm of hungry ghosts, and (3) the realm of animals.

three poisons: Desire, aversion, and delusion, all of which hinder the pursuit of enlightenment.

three vehicles: The three paths to enlightenment—(1) the *srāvaka* vehicle, (2) the *pratyekabuddha* vehicle, and (3) the bodhisattva vehicle, otherwise known as the Mahayana. See also bodhisattva; Mahayana; *pratyekabuddha; śrāvaka*.

Tripiṭaka: The three categories of the Buddhist canon—(1) Sutra, the Buddha's sermons, (2) Vinaya, the rules of conduct for monks and nuns, and (3) Abhidharma, commentaries on the Buddha's teachings.

Bibliography

Nichiren. *St. Nichiren's Kaimoku-sho: Open Your Eyes to the Lotus Teaching*. Translated by Kyotsu Hori. Tokyo: Nichirenshu Overseas Propagation Promotion Association, 1987.

Nichiren. *The Major Writings of Nichiren Daishonin*. Translated by The Seikyo Times. Tokyo: Nichiren Shoshu International Center, 1979–90.

Nichiren. "Kaimokusho." In *La doctrine de Nichiren*. Translated by C. Renondeau. Paris: Presses Universitaires de France, 1953.

Nichiren. *The Awakening to the Truth, or, Kaimokusho*. Translated by N. R. M. Ehara. Tokyo: International Buddhist Society, 1941.

Index

A

Abhidharma 85
Āgama sutras 14, 20, 30, 34, 52, 53, 57, 69, 89
Age of Conflicts 45, 46
Age of the Counterfeit of the Right Teachings of the Buddha 45, 46, 48, 98, 99, 100, 102–103, 105, 108
Age of Degeneration 28, 38, 41, 43, 45, 46, 47, 48, 92, 95, 98–99, 100, 103, 104, 108, 122, 123, 125
Age of the Right Teachings of the Buddha 38, 98, 100, 101, 102
Ajātaśatru, King 44, 53, 54, 68, 91
Ajita, King 53, 66
Akṣobhya 120
ālaya-vijñāna 87
Amitābha 72
Amoghavajra 37, 75, 83
Āmravana 54
Ānanda 18, 50, 53, 101
Anantacāritra 64
Anavatapta Pond 81, 112
anuttara-samyak-saṁbodhi 22, 30, 32, 66, 67, 68
arhat(s), arhatship 18, 21, 22, 47, 50, 51, 52, 95, 97, 98, 105
Asaṅga 35, 36, 91
Aśoka, King 48
asura(s) 23, 32, 68, 81, 112, 120
Aśvaghoṣa 101
Avataṁsaka Sect. *See* Kegon Sect
Avataṁsaka-sūtra 16, 19, 26, 28, 29, 30, 31, 32, 34, 36, 37, 57, 58, 61, 62, 64, 66, 67, 69, 70, 74, 76, 77, 82, 83, 85, 88, 89, 104
Ayodhya 35

B

Bhaiṣajyaguru 71
Bhaiṣajyrāja 126
bhikṣu(s) (*see also* monk; priest) 15, 47, 55, 95–96, 97, 98, 101, 102, 103, 105, 112, 123, 124
Bimbisāra, King 68
bodhi 87, 88, 113
Bodhidharma 45, 106, 107, 108
bodhisattva(s) 12, 23, 25, 26, 27, 29, 31, 41, 43, 45, 47, 48, 56, 57, 58, 59, 61, 62, 63, 64, 65, 66, 67, 68, 70, 71, 76, 77, 83, 91, 92, 93, 95, 97, 98, 99, 100, 101, 102, 105, 102, 113, 114, 117, 126
bodhi tree 30, 66
Book of Filial Piety 93
Brahma(s) 25, 49, 52, 54, 57, 62, 70, 71, 117, 118
Brahma Heaven 13, 117, 118
brahman(s) 11, 12, 14, 24, 35, 43, 44, 45, 47, 53, 58, 92, 96, 98, 105, 108, 114, 125
Brahmanism, Brahmanist 7, 10–12, 14, 18, 42, 54, 58, 84, 104
Buddhahood 2, 18, 21, 22, 30, 31, 32, 33, 34, 37, 41, 42, 50, 51, 55, 56, 59, 61, 62, 64, 71, 73, 74, 75, 77, 91, 92, 93, 112, 114, 118, 119, 123
Buddha-nature 14, 19, 20, 36, 85, 89, 90
Buddha vehicle 61, 76
Buddha worlds 28, 33, 61, 62, 81, 88, 92

C

Candraprabha 68, 71
Chang-an 117, 118, 123, 124, 125

Ch'ao-kao 74
Chao-wang, King 100
Ch'en dynasty 16, 46, 106
Ch'eng-kuan 16, 37, 70, 74, 76, 82, 89, 91
Chia-hsiang 75, 89, 91
Chia-shang 35, 70
Chi-cha 49
Chieh, King 50, 113
Ch'i-fu 76
Chih-che. *See* T'ien-t'ai
Chih-i 44
Chih-tu 44, 96, 98, 101, 108
Chih-yen 37, 82
China 7, 10, 14, 16, 17, 35, 36, 37, 38, 44, 67, 74, 75, 81, 82, 90, 99, 100, 106, 107, 118, 126
Ch'in dynasty 115
Chi-tsang 60, 82
Chou dynasty 7, 9, 100
Chou, King 7, 50, 113
Chou-kung 8
Chuang-tzu 8, 15
Ch'ung-hua 7
Chung-ni 10
Chu-tao-sheng 112
Ciñcā 53
Confucianism 7–10, 11, 12, 14, 15, 18, 20, 42, 84, 92, 100, 101
Confucius 8, 9, 12

D

Daiju-kinnara-kyō 85
Daimoku faith 1
Dainichi 123
Daiun-kyō 85, 89
Daṇḍapāṇi 112
Daśabhūmivibhāṣā-śāstra 83
Deer Park 52
Delight Dharma Bodhisattva 126
Dengyō 17, 28, 36, 37, 45, 46, 47, 61, 73, 75, 76, 77, 81, 83, 91, 99, 102, 103, 108, 125, 126
Deva 68, 112, 126
Devadatta 47, 53, 54, 68, 81, 91, 92, 93, 110
Devarāja (*see also* Devadatta) 91, 92
devil(s) 17, 24, 30, 42, 45, 68, 96, 116
dhāraṇī(s) 85–86, 90
Dharma Cloud Freedom King 60
Dharmalakṣaṇa Sect. *See* Hossō Sect
Dharma-nature 87
Dharmapāla 35
Dharma Wisdom Bodhisattva 57, 58, 63, 66
Dharma world 89
*dhātu*s, two 71, 74
  garbhadhātu 75
  vajradhātu 75
dhyāna(s) 20
Dōji 35
Dōkyō 74
Dōshō 35, 112
dragon(s) 23, 48, 55, 57, 59, 65, 80, 81, 82, 90, 91, 92
Droṇodana, King 50, 53

E

Eightfold Path 107
Emancipation Moon Bodhisattva 57
Enchin 84
Encho 75
Eshin 103
evil regions (*see also* hell) 39, 42, 48, 118
  three 11, 23, 54, 55

F

Fa-tao 112
Fa-tsang 37, 73, 82
F'ei-kung 81
Five Elders 9
five kinds of living beings 44–45
five sins. *See under* sin
five *skandha*s 116
five tastes, simile of 52, 59, 86, 88–89, 90, 104

five virtues 3, 9
four kinds of devotees 79, 112
Four Noble Truths 86, 107
Four Saints 8, 12, 64
four teachings (*see also* Hinayana; Mahayana, -cum-Hinayana, Specialized, Perfect) 33, 57, 59, 104
Four Vedas 10
Fuhōzō-kyō 48, 101

G

Ganges River 11, 13, 38, 43, 52, 59, 80, 117
*garbhadhātu. See under dhātu*s
garuḍa(s) 81, 112
gāthā(s) 43, 80, 126
Gautama 44, 53, 54
Gayā 32, 66, 67, 68
Gentle Face Bodhisattva 57
Ghanavyūha-sūtra 85, 90
god(s) 2, 9, 10, 11, 17, 22, 23, 24, 32, 45, 46, 47, 49, 52, 53, 54–55, 56, 57, 58, 59, 61, 62, 68, 71, 72, 76, 77, 80, 86, 91, 109, 113, 114, 119, 120
Gomyō 108
Great Adornment Bodhisattva 67
Great Vehicle (*see also* Mahayana) 12, 14, 86, 87, 88

H

Han dynasty (*see also* Later Han dynasty) 7, 50, 64
Hatsunaion-gyō 97, 105, 107, 115
heaven(s) 10, 11, 13, 20, 23, 25, 70, 82
Heavenly Kings of the Four Quarters 62, 71
Heavenly Venerables 7, 8
Heizei, Emperor 46
hell(s) 48, 85, 106, 113, 114, 118
Hell of Incessant Suffering 21, 42, 113, 118, 120, 124
Hieizan Enryakuji Temple 17
Himalaya Mountains 19
Hinayana (*see also* Lesser Vehicle; Mahayana, -cum-Hinayana) 13, 26, 27, 33, 38, 41, 42, 45, 48, 57, 58, 92, 103, 104
Hitomaro 75
Hōdōarani-kyō 22
Hokekyō. See Saddharma-puṇḍarīka-sūtra
Hokke-gengi 60
Hokke-genron 75
Hokke-genzan-yōshū 76
Hokkemongu-ki 96, 102, 121
Hokke-sandaibu-fuchū 106
Hokke-shūku 45, 73
Hōmetsujin-kyō 38
Hōnen 42, 102, 103, 104, 123, 125
Hō-on-girinjō 76
Hossō Sect 13, 14, 16, 27, 29, 35, 36, 76, 82, 84, 89, 91, 119
Hsia dynasty 50, 113
Hsiang-yü 81
Hsi-wang-mu, Queen 81
Hsüan-tsang 16, 35, 36, 82
Huang emperors, three 3, 7, 72, 84
Hui-neng 108
Hui-ti, Emperor 64

I

icchantika(s) 20, 30, 61, 85, 91, 92, 97, 98, 105, 107, 113, 122
Ichinosawa 1
I-hsing 75
I-kung, King 8
India 10, 16, 23, 35, 36, 37, 38, 45, 46, 48, 58, 60, 82

J

Jambudvīpa 19, 54, 97
Japan 16, 17, 28, 35, 36, 38, 42, 67, 73, 75, 81, 82, 83, 90, 91, 100, 101, 103, 104, 109, 114, 116, 118, 122, 125
Jikaku 85
Jinzū-kyō 85

Jitsu-e 75
Jīvaka 68
Jōdo Sect 17, 72, 77
Jōjitsu Sect 4, 13, 14, 72
Jūji-kyō 85

K

Kālodāyin 54
Kamakura District 2
Kamakura government 1
Kammu, Emperor 46
Kammuryōju-kyō 68, 77, 104, 114
Kapila (*see also* Three Seers) 10
Kāśyapa 10, 18, 19, 20, 23, 24, 44, 49, 52, 54, 55, 56, 68, 101, 103, 108, 113, 122, 123
Kātyāyana 18
Kegon Sect 4, 13, 16, 27, 29, 36, 37, 60, 70, 72, 73, 74, 75, 76, 82, 84, 89, 91, 119
Kenkairon 45
Kōbō 17, 70, 75, 76, 83, 89, 90, 91
Kōjō 75
Kokuri 67
Kośa Sect. *See* Kusha Sect
Kuang-t'ung 45
Kuang-wu-ti, Emperor 9
K'uei-chi 35
Kumārajīva 126
Kung-yin 8, 49
K'un-ming 50
Kusha Sect 4, 13, 14, 72

L

Laṅkāvatāra-sūtra 82
Lao-tzu 8, 10, 15
Later Han dynasty (*see also* Han dynasty) 9, 16, 84, 100, 106
lay followers, supporters 15, 43, 53
layman, laymen 17, 39, 79, 45, 53, 96, 101, 109, 121
laywoman, laywomen 39, 79
Lesser Vehicle (*see also* Hinayana) 21
Liang-hsü 75
Light-Pure Bodhisattva 10
Lotus King world 29
Lotus Store world 62
Lotus Sutra (*see also Saddharma-puṇḍarīka-sūtra*) 1, 2, 4

M

Madhyāntika 48
Magadha 44, 59
Mahābhijñājñānābhibhū 41, 114
Mahākaruṇā-sūtra 48
Mahāmāyā-sūtra 48
Mahāparinirvāṇa-sūtra 2, 11, 28, 35, 36, 38, 42, 44, 59, 68, 82, 88, 89, 90, 91, 97, 98, 102, 103, 105, 112, 113, 117, 120, 121, 122, 124
Mahāprajāpati 18
Mahāprajñāpāramitā-śāstra 60
Mahāprajñāpāramitā-sūtra 22, 26, 30, 32, 34, 61, 63, 82, 87, 89, 104
Mahāsaṁnipāta-sūtra 20, 26, 30, 63, 69
Mahāvairocana 37, 63, 71, 72, 83, 87
Mahāvairocana-sūtra 16, 28, 30, 32, 34, 37, 61, 63, 64, 69, 70, 71, 74, 75, 77, 82, 83, 87
Mahayana (*see also* Great Vehicle) 13, 26, 27, 35, 38, 41, 45, 61, 72, 74, 85, 88, 92, 97, 116
- -cum-Hinayana 33, 57, 58
- Perfect 33, 57, 58, 103–104
- Provisional 16, 34, 42, 70, 74, 84
- Specialized 33, 57, 58, 103
- True 42, 84

Maheśvara 10
Maitreya 32, 35, 36, 64, 65, 66, 67, 68, 91
Makashikan 10, 15, 74, 102, 103, 106, 107, 116, 120
mandala(s) 74, 75
Mañjuśrī 21, 22, 25, 58, 64, 83, 117
mantra(s) 16, 60, 74, 85

Many Treasures Buddha 25, 79, 80
Mao-pao 50
Māra 27, 97, 103
māras 45, 52, 116
Maudgalyāyana 2, 18, 44, 54, 112
Medicine King Bodhisattva 99
Merits Forest Bodhisattva 57
Miao-le 2, 9, 36, 44, 61, 66, 72, 73, 84, 98, 101, 103, 106, 107, 122
Middle Way 119
Ming-ti, Emperor 100, 106
monk(s) (*see also bhikṣu;* priest) 21, 79, 103, 109, 121, 122
Moonlight Bodhisattva 10
Moriya 110
Mo-t'a 38
Mount Gṛdhrakūṭa 53
Mount Sacred Eagle 50, 59, 62, 64, 65, 71, 90, 98, 120
Mount Shang-shan 64
Mount Sumeru 28, 42, 56, 80, 89, 91
mudra(s) 16, 74, 85
Muemutoku-daijōshiron-gengi-ki 60
Munemori 81
Muryōgi-kyō 30, 31, 55, 59, 67, 69
Myōhōrenge-kyō (*see also Saddharmapuṇḍarīka-sūtra*) 3, 48, 60, 98

N

Nāgārjuna 14, 48, 60, 83, 90, 101
NAGASAKI Yoritsuna 1
Namu-myōhōrenge-kyō (*see also Myōhōrenge-kyō*) 60
Nanda 35
Nara, sects of 17, 45, 46, 48, 99, 125
Nehangyō-sho 121
Nembutsu Sect 27, 79, 93, 98, 104, 108, 109, 120, 123, 124, 125
Nen-a 108
Never Despising Bodhisattva 44, 111, 112, 122
Nichiren 1–2, 81, 91, 95, 109
nine easinesses, sutras of 42, 82, 83, 89, 91
Ninnō-hannya-kyō 30, 69
nirmaṇakāya. See under trikāya
nirvana 11, 20, 79, 86, 87, 113
nun(s) 39, 79

O

one mind–three thousand, teaching of 13–14, 16, 32, 33, 34, 59, 62, 74, 76, 92, 119, 124
One Vehicle 31, 45, 76, 103, 112

P

Padmaprabha (*see also* Śāriputra) 18, 19, 55, 101
Pai-chü-i 112
pāramitā(s) 60
parinirvāṇa 12, 13, 55, 91
Pārśva 101
P'ei-kung 7
Pekche 37, 67
Pi-kan 7
Prabhūtaratna 13, 19, 24, 31, 62, 64, 65, 81, 95, 99, 101, 104, 109, 124
prajña 87
Prajñāpāramitā sutras 57, 58, 64, 70, 76, 85
Prasenajit, King 54
pratyekabuddha 20
pratyekabuddha vehicle (*see also* two vehicles) 18, 88
precepts 9, 15, 20, 49, 53, 98, 103, 105, 118, 121, 122, 123
  five 11, 120, 123
  ten 11
priest(s) (*see also bhikṣu;* monk) 15, 16, 17, 23, 27, 28, 39, 42, 45, 46, 47, 48, 54, 79, 84, 85, 106, 109, 125
P'u-kuang 35
Pure World(s) 26, 65, 70, 73, 118, 120
Pūrṇa 18, 52

R

Rāhula 18, 50, 121
rākṣasa, rākṣasīs 77, 113
Raśmiprabhāsa (*see also* Kāśyapa) 18, 19, 55, 101
Ratnaviśuddha world 24
Replica-Buddhas 62, 64, 65, 80, 99, 101, 109, 124
Risshō-ankoku-ron 114
Ritsu Sect 4, 13, 14, 47, 48, 72, 93, 98
Ropparamitsu-kyō 85, 90
Ṛṣabha (*see also* Three Seers) 10
Ryōkan 108

S

Saddharmapuṇḍarīka-sūtra 4, 7, 12, 13–14, 17, 18, 19, 24, 25, 26, 27, 28, 31, 32, 33, 34, 35, 36, 37, 38, 42, 43, 46, 47, 48, 49, 50, 51, 55, 56, 60, 61, 63, 69, 70, 71, 74, 75, 76, 77, 81, 82, 83, 84, 85, 89, 90, 91, 92, 93, 101, 103, 104, 105, 108, 109, 112, 113, 114, 115, 116, 118, 119, 120, 121, 123, 125
  "Chapter on Beholding the Stupa of Treasures" 42, 62, 63, 64, 79, 91, 124
  "Chapter on Bodhisattvas from Underground" 31, 34, 35
  "Chapter on Devadatta" 68, 81, 91
  "Chapter on the Duration of the Life of the Tathāgata" 14, 30, 32, 34, 35, 37, 63, 68, 70–71, 72, 73
  "Chapter on Encouragement of Expounding the Dharma" 99
  "Chapter on Encouragement of Keeping the Sutra" 47, 93, 95
  "Chapter on Expedients" 33, 59, 69
  "Chapter on Never Despising Bodhisattva" 111, 112, 122
  "Chapter on Peaceful Practices" 69, 98, 103, 120, 122
  "Chapter on the Previous Life of Medicine King Bodhisattva" 99
  "Chapter on the Variety of Merits" 99
  "Discourse of the Historical Buddha" 33, 34, 90
  "Discourse of the Original Buddha" 14, 33, 34, 24, 90
  enemies of 48, 79, 99–110, 111
  hatred of 43–46, 56
  practitioner(s) of 41, 47, 48, 49, 51, 52, 55, 56, 77, 100, 109, 110, 111, 112, 116
Sado Island 1, 95
Saga, Emperor 46
Sāgaravaradharabuddhivikrīḍitābhijña (*see also* Ānanda) 18, 50
Sahā world 24, 25, 32, 51, 62, 63, 64, 66, 70, 79, 124
Śakra 11, 49, 54, 62, 64, 68, 71, 81, 112
Śākyamuni 13, 19, 24, 25, 26, 29, 32-33, 34, 37, 41, 57, 58, 62, 63, 64, 65, 66, 67, 68, 69, 70, 71, 72, 77, 79, 81, 90, 95, 99, 101, 104, 125, 126
Śākyas 32, 67, 68
samādhi 22, 56
  sea emblem 30
  śūraṁgama 22
Samantabhadra 64, 83
Samantaprabhāsa 18
sambhogakāya. See under trikāya
Saṁdhinirmocana-sūtra 61, 82, 86
Sannō 17
Sanron Sect 13, 14, 16, 27, 29, 36, 75, 82, 89, 91, 119
Saptaratnapadmavikrāntagāmin (*see also* Rāhula) 18, 50
Śāraṅganātha Grove 86
Śāriputra 18, 19, 20, 22, 23, 24, 27, 28, 44, 49, 52, 54, 55, 59, 61, 101, 114

Sarvatathāgatatattvasaṁgraha 63, 64, 71, 75
Sattaramafundarikya-sotaran (*see also Saddharmapuṇḍarīka-sūtra*) 60
Satyasiddhi Sect. *See* Jōjitsu Sect
sect(s) (*see also* Hossō; Jōdo; Jōjitsu; Kegon; Kusha; Nembutsu; Ritsu; Sanron; Shingon; Tendai; Tendai Hokke; Vaipulya; Vatsīputrīya; Yuishiki; Zen)
  eight 17
  seven 17, 77
  seven, of North China 16, 44, 46, 48, 99, 125
  six, of Nara. *See* Nara, sects of
  three, of South China 16, 44, 46, 48, 99, 125
Seer Prophet, King 120
Senchaku-hongan-nembutsu-shū 103
Shan-tao 42
Shen-fang 35
Shijo Kingo 2
Shikan-guketsu 10, 15, 106, 107, 120
Shinga 75
Shingon Sect 13, 16, 17, 27, 29, 36, 37, 70, 73, 74, 75, 77, 84, 85, 89, 91, 109, 119, 123, 126
Shinjikan-gyō 112
Shi-po 7
Shō Hachiman 17
Shōhoke-kyō (*see also Saddharma-puṇḍarīka-sūtra*) 3, 48, 60, 99
Shōjō-hōgyō-kyō 10
Shōmu, Emperor 35
Shōtoku, Crown Prince 67, 110, 126
Shuen 108
Shun-wang, King 8
Siddhārtha, Crown Prince 29
Śīlabhadra 35
Śīlāditya, King 35
Silla 37
sin(s) 1, 68, 86, 91, 92, 112, 113, 116, 117, 118
  eight grave 85
  five 21, 22, 85, 92, 118
  four grave 85
  seven 92
Siṁha 2, 112, 126
Siṁhahunu, King 29
six difficulties, sutras of 42, 82, 83, 89, 91
skandhas. *See* five *skandhas*
śrāvaka(s) 18, 20, 22, 23, 24, 27, 49–50, 51–55, 71, 73, 98, 101, 105
śravaka vehicle (*see also* two vehicles) 18, 86, 88
Śrīmālāsiṁhanāda-sūtra 85
storehouse consciousness. *See* *ālaya-vijñāna*
storehouses of the Dharma 13, 15, 85–86
stupa(s) 24–25, 52, 62, 79, 80, 99
Śubhākarasiṁha 16, 37, 60, 73, 74, 75, 76, 83
Subhūti 18, 22, 52, 54, 55
Śuddhodana, King 29, 50
Sui dynasty 16, 46
Sukhāvatīvyūha-sūtra 26, 28, 63
Sumeru world(s) 26, 52, 88
Sunakkhatta 91
Superior Truth-Born Bodhisattva 86
Supratiṣṭhitacāritra 64
Śūraṁgama-sūtra 22
Sūryaprabhāsana 71
Sutra 85
Sutra of the Lotus Flower of the Wonderful Dharma (*see also Saddharmapuṇḍarīka-sūtra*) 25, 79, 84
Sutra of Twelve Elements (*see also Avataṁsaka-sūtra*) 89
Suvarṇaprabhāsa-sūtra 10, 26, 34, 63, 114
Su-yu, Prime Minister 100

T

T'ai-kung-wang 8, 64
T'ai-tsung, Emperor 35
T'ang dynasty 73
Tao-ch'o 42, 102, 103
Taoism 14, 15
Tatsunokuchi 1
Ta-t'zu-en-ssu Temple 35
Tembon-myōhōrenge-kyō 3, 99
Tendai Hokke Sect 4, 73, 108
Tendai Sect 4, 16, 17, 29, 71, 72, 75, 76, 84, 106, 109, 119, 123, 125
Tenjin 112
Tenshō Daijin 17
three obstacles 42, 116, 117
three poisons 12, 21, 107
Three Śāstras Sect. *See* Sanron Sect
Three Seers 10, 12, 58
three vehicles 31, 32, 76
Ti emperors, five 3, 7, 84
T'ien-t'ai 4, 10, 14, 16, 17, 34, 36, 37, 44, 46, 47, 63, 65, 74, 76, 83, 90, 91, 99, 107, 112, 122, 123, 125, 126
T'ien-t'ai Saddharmapuṇḍarīka Sect. *See* Tendai Hokke Sect
T'ien-t'ai Sect. *See* Tendai Sect
Ting-lan 7
Toji Temple 17
Tokuichi 44, 125
trikāya(s) 35, 63
  dharmakāya 35, 83, 122
  nirmāṇakāya(s) 35, 63, 70, 72
  sambhogakāya(s) 35, 62, 70, 83
Tripiṭaka 4, 36, 51
Ts'u-e 16
Tsukahara 1, 2
Tu-shun 37, 82
Tuṣita Heaven 35
two vehicles (*see also pratyekabuddha* vehicle; *śravaka* vehicle) 19–24, 26, 28, 30, 32, 33, 34, 36, 37, 45, 55, 62, 74, 75, 76
Tz'u-en 36, 70, 76, 82, 89, 91

U

Ulūka (*see also* Three Seers) 10
Utpalavarṇā 54

V

Vaidehī, Queen 68
Vaipulya Sect 38, 84
Vaipulya sutras 30, 34, 57, 58, 61, 64, 70, 82, 88, 89, 97, 98, 105
Vairocana 70, 72
Vajra Banner Bodhisattva 57
Vajrabodhi 16, 37, 83
*vajradhatu. See under dhātu*s
Vajrapāṇi 87
Vajrasattva 64
Vajra Store Bodhisattva 57
Vārāṇasī 86
Vasubandhu 14, 35, 36, 74
Vātsīputrīya Sect 38, 84
Vijñaptimātra Sect. *See* Yuishiki Sect
Vimalakīrti 21, 69
Vimalakīrtinirdeśa-sūtra 21, 23, 30, 54, 69
Vinaya 85
Vinaya Sect. *See* Ritsu Sect
Virūḍhaka, King 54
Viśiṣṭacāritra 64
Viṣṇu 10
Viśuddhacāritra 64

W

Wang-yin 49
Wei-yüan-sung 15
Wen-wang, King 8
women, possibility of their attaining Buddhahood 92, 93
world(s)
  of the four quarters 26, 63
  of the six quarters 26, 77
  of the ten quarters 13, 14, 23, 24, 25, 26, 27, 28, 51, 57, 63, 64, 65, 66, 70, 71, 80, 82, 95, 99, 101, 104, 124
  triple 20, 23, 49, 55

wrong views 12, 14, 15, 19, 43, 76, 96, 98, 103, 105, 108, 115, 122
Wu-ch'eng 8
Wu-kou 38
Wu-ti, Emperor 50
Wu-wang, King 7, 9

Y

Yama 75
Yamashina-dera Temple 36
Yao-wang, King 8
Yaśodharā 18
Yeh-lo 107
Yen-hui 10
Yin dynasty 7, 50, 113
Yin-shou 8
Yōmei, Emperor 67
Yoritomo 81
Yuishiki Sect (*see also* Hossō Sect) 4, 82
Yung-p'ing 16

Z

Zen Sect 17, 72, 79, 93, 98, 106, 107, 108, 109, 120, 123, 124, 125

A List of the Volumes of the BDK English Tripiṭaka (First Series)

Abbreviations

Ch.: Chinese
Skt.: Sanskrit
Jp.: Japanese
Eng.: Published title
T.: Taishō Tripiṭaka

Vol. No.		Title	*T.* No.
1, 2	*Ch.*	Ch'ang-a-han-ching (長阿含經)	1
	Skt.	Dīrghāgama	
3–8	*Ch.*	Chung-a-han-ching (中阿含經)	26
	Skt.	Madhyamāgama	
9-I	*Ch.*	Ta-ch'eng-pên-shêng-hsin-ti-kuan-ching (大乘本生心地觀經)	159
9-II	*Ch.*	Fo-so-hsing-tsan (佛所行讃)	192
	Skt.	Buddhacarita	
10-I	*Ch.*	Tsa-pao-ts'ang-ching (雜寶藏經)	203
	Eng.	The Storehouse of Sundry Valuables	
10-II	*Ch.*	Fa-chü-p'i-yü-ching (法句譬喩經)	211
	Eng.	The Scriptural Text: Verses of the Doctrine, with Parables	
11-I	*Ch.*	Hsiao-p'in-pan-jo-po-lo-mi-ching (小品般若波羅蜜經)	227
	Skt.	Aṣṭasāhasrikā-prajñāpāramitā-sūtra	
11-II	*Ch.*	Chin-kang-pan-jo-po-lo-mi-ching (金剛般若波羅蜜經)	235
	Skt.	Vajracchedikā-prajñāpāramitā-sūtra	

Vol. No.		Title	*T.* No.
11-III	*Ch.*	Jên-wang-pan-jo-po-lo-mi-ching (仁王般若波羅蜜經)	245
	Skt.	Kāruṇikārājā-prajñāpāramitā-sūtra (?)	
11-IV	*Ch.*	Pan-jo-po-lo-mi-to-hsing-ching (般若波羅蜜多心經)	251
	Skt.	Prajñāpāramitāhṛdaya-sūtra	
12-I	*Ch.*	Ta-lo-chin-kang-pu-k'ung-chên-shih-san-mo-yeh-ching (大樂金剛不空眞實三麼耶經)	243
	Skt.	Adhyardhaśatikā-prajñāpāramitā-sūtra	
12-II	*Ch.*	Wu-liang-shou-ching (無量壽經)	360
	Skt.	Sukhāvatīvyūha	
	Eng.	The Larger Sutra on Amitāyus (In The Three Pure Land Sutras)	
12-III	*Ch.*	Kuan-wu-liang-shou-fo-ching (觀無量壽佛經)	365
	Skt.	Amitāyurdhyāna-sūtra	
	Eng.	The Sutra on Contemplation of Amitāyus (In The Three Pure Land Sutras)	
12-IV	*Ch.*	A-mi-t'o-ching (阿彌陀經)	366
	Skt.	Sukhāvatīvyūha	
	Eng.	The Smaller Sutra on Amitāyus (In The Three Pure Land Sutras)	
12-V	*Ch.*	Ti-ts'ang-p'u-sa-pên-yüan-ching (地藏菩薩本願經)	412
	Skt.	Kṣitigarbhapraṇidhāna-sūtra (?)	
12-VI	*Ch.*	Yao-shih-liu-li-kuang-ju-lai-pên-yüan-kung-tê-ching (藥師琉璃光如來本願功德經)	450
	Skt.	Bhaiṣajyaguruvaiḍūryaprabhāsapūrva-praṇidhānaviśeṣavistara	
12-VII	*Ch.*	Mi-lê-hsia-shêng-ch'êng-fo-ching (彌勒下生成佛經)	454
	Skt.	Maitreyavyākaraṇa (?)	
12-VIII	*Ch.*	Wên-shu-shih-li-wên-ching (文殊師利問經)	468
	Skt.	Mañjuśrīparipṛcchā (?)	
13-I	*Ch.*	Miao-fa-lien-hua-ching (妙法蓮華經)	262
	Skt.	Saddharmapuṇḍarīka-sūtra	
	Eng.	The Lotus Sutra	
13-II	*Ch.*	Wu-liang-i-ching (無量義經)	276

Vol. No.		Title	*T.* No.
13-III	*Ch.*	Kuan-p'u-hsien-p'u-sa-hsing-fa-ching (觀普賢菩薩行法經)	277
14–19	*Ch.*	Ta-fang-kuang-fo-hua-yen-ching (大方廣佛華嚴經)	278
	Skt.	Avataṃsaka-sūtra	
20-I	*Ch.*	Shêng-man-shih-tzŭ-hou-i-ch'eng-ta-fang-pien-fang-kuang-ching (勝鬘師子吼一乘大方便方廣經)	353
	Skt.	Śrīmālādevīsiṃhanāda-sūtra	
20-II	*Ch.*	Chin-kuang-ming-tsui-shêng-wang-ching (金光明最勝王經)	665
	Skt.	Suvarṇaprabhāsa-sūtra	
21–24	*Ch.*	Ta-pan-nieh-p'an-ching (大般涅槃經)	374
	Skt.	Mahāparinirvāṇa-sūtra	
25-I	*Ch.*	Fo-ch'ui-pan-nieh-p'an-liao-shuo-chiao-chieh-ching (佛垂般涅槃略説教誡經)	389
25-II	*Ch.*	Pan-chou-san-mei-ching (般舟三昧經)	418
	Skt.	Pratyutpannabuddhasammukhāvasthitasamādhi-sūtra	
	Eng.	The Pratyutpanna Samādhi Sutra	
25-III	*Ch.*	Shou-lêng-yen-san-mei-ching (首楞嚴三昧經)	642
	Skt.	Śūraṅgamasamādhi-sūtra	
	Eng.	The Śūraṅgama Samādhi Sutra	
25-IV	*Ch.*	Chieh-shên-mi-ching (解深密經)	676
	Skt.	Saṃdhinirmocana-sūtra	
	Eng.	The Scripture on the Explication of Underlying Meaning	
25-V	*Ch.*	Yü-lan-p'ên-ching (盂蘭盆經)	685
	Skt.	Ullambana-sūtra (?)	
25-VI	*Ch.*	Ssŭ-shih-êrh-chang-ching (四十二章經)	784
26-I	*Ch.*	Wei-mo-chieh-so-shuo-ching (維摩詰所説經)	475
	Skt.	Vimalakīrtinirdeśa-sūtra	
26-II	*Ch.*	Yüeh-shang-nü-ching (月上女經)	480
	Skt.	Candrottarādārikāparipṛcchā	

Vol. No.		Title	*T.* No.
26-III	*Ch.*	Tso-ch'an-san-mei-ching (坐禪三昧經)	614
26-IV	*Ch.* *Skt.*	Ta-mo-to-lo-ch'an-ching (達磨多羅禪經) Yogācārabhūmi-sūtra (?)	618
27	*Ch.* *Skt.*	Yüeh-têng-san-mei-ching (月燈三昧經) Samādhirājacandrapradīpa-sūtra	639
28	*Ch.* *Skt.*	Ju-lêng-ch'ieh-ching (入楞伽經) Laṅkāvatāra-sūtra	671
29-I	*Ch.*	Ta-fang-kuang-yüan-chio-hsiu-to-lo-liao-i-ching (大方廣圓覺修多羅了義經)	842
29-II	*Ch.* *Skt.*	Su-hsi-ti-chieh-lo-ching (蘇悉地羯囉經) Susiddhikaramahātantrasādhanopāyika-paṭala	893
29-III	*Ch.* *Skt.*	Mo-têng-ch'ieh-ching (摩登伽經) Mātaṅgī-sūtra (?)	1300
30-I	*Ch.* *Skt.*	Ta-p'i-lu-chê-na-chêng-fo-shên-pien-chia-ch'ih-ching (大毘盧遮那成佛神變加持經) Mahāvairocanābhisambodhivikurvitādhiṣṭhāna-vaipulyasūtrendrarāja-nāma-dharmaparyāya	848
30-II	*Ch.* *Skt.*	Ching-kang-ting-i-ch'ieh-ju-lai-chên-shih-shê-ta-ch'eng-hsien-chêng-ta-chiao-wang-ching (金剛頂一切如來眞實攝大乘現證大教王經) Sarvatathāgatatattvasaṃgrahamahāyānābhi-samayamahākalparāja	865
31–35	*Ch.* *Skt.*	Mo-ho-sêng-ch'i-lü (摩訶僧祇律) Mahāsāṃghika-vinaya (?)	1425
36–42	*Ch.* *Skt.*	Ssŭ-fên-lü (四分律) Dharmaguptaka-vinaya (?)	1428
43, 44	*Ch.* *Pāli*	Shan-chien-lü-p'i-p'o-sha (善見律毘婆沙) Samantapāsādikā	1462
45-I	*Ch.* *Skt.*	Fan-wang-ching (梵網經) Brahmajāla-sūtra (?)	1484
45-II	*Ch.* *Skt.* *Eng.*	Yu-p'o-sai-chieh-ching (優婆塞戒經) Upāsakaśīla-sūtra (?) The Sutra on Upāsaka Precepts	1488

Vol. No.		Title	T. No.
46-I	*Ch.*	Miao-fa-lien-hua-ching-yu-po-t'i-shê (妙法蓮華經憂波提舍)	1519
	Skt.	Saddharmapuṇḍarīka-upadeśa	
46-II	*Ch.*	Fo-ti-ching-lun (佛地經論)	1530
	Skt.	Buddhabhūmisūtra-śāstra (?)	
46-III	*Ch.*	Shê-ta-ch'eng-lun (攝大乘論)	1593
	Skt.	Mahāyānasaṃgraha	
	Eng.	The Summary of the Great Vehicle	
47	*Ch.*	Shih-chu-p'i-p'o-sha-lun (十住毘婆沙論)	1521
	Skt.	Daśabhūmika-vibhāṣā (?)	
48, 49	*Ch.*	A-p'i-ta-mo-chü-shê-lun (阿毘達磨倶舍論)	1558
	Skt.	Abhidharmakośa-bhāṣya	
50–59	*Ch.*	Yü-ch'ieh-shih-ti-lun (瑜伽師地論)	1579
	Skt.	Yogācārabhūmi	
60-I	*Ch.*	Ch'êng-wei-shih-lun (成唯識論)	1585
	Eng.	Demonstration of Consciousness Only (In Three Texts on Consciousness Only)	
60-II	*Ch.*	Wei-shih-san-shih-lun-sung (唯識三十論頌)	1586
	Skt.	Triṃśikā	
	Eng.	The Thirty Verses on Consciousness Only (In Three Texts on Consciousness Only)	
60-III	*Ch.*	Wei-shih-êrh-shih-lun (唯識二十論)	1590
	Skt.	Viṃśatikā	
	Eng.	The Treatise in Twenty Verses on Consciousness Only (In Three Texts on Consciousness Only)	
61-I	*Ch.*	Chung-lun (中論)	1564
	Skt.	Madhyamaka-śāstra	
61-II	*Ch.*	Pien-chung-pien-lun (辯中邊論)	1600
	Skt.	Madhyāntavibhāga	
61-III	*Ch.*	Ta-ch'eng-ch'êng-yeh-lun (大乘成業論)	1609
	Skt.	Karmasiddhiprakaraṇa	
61-IV	*Ch.*	Yin-ming-ju-chêng-li-lun (因明入正理論)	1630
	Skt.	Nyāyapraveśa	

Vol. No.		Title	*T.* No.
61-V	*Ch.*	Chin-kang-chên-lun (金剛針論)	1642
	Skt.	Vajrasūcī	
61-VI	*Ch.*	Chang-so-chih-lun (彰所知論)	1645
62	*Ch.*	Ta-ch'eng-chuang-yen-ching-lun (大乘莊嚴經論)	1604
	Skt.	Mahāyānasūtrālaṃkāra	
63-I	*Ch.*	Chiu-ching-i-ch'eng-pao-hsing-lun (究竟一乘寳性論)	1611
	Skt.	Ratnagotravibhāgamahāyānottaratantra-śāstra	
63-II	*Ch.*	P'u-t'i-hsing-ching (菩提行經)	1662
	Skt.	Bodhicaryāvatāra	
63-III	*Ch.*	Chin-kang-ting-yü-ch'ieh-chung-fa-a-nou-to-lo-san-miao-san-p'u-t'i-hsin-lun (金剛頂瑜伽中發阿耨多羅三藐三菩提心論)	1665
63-IV	*Ch.*	Ta-ch'eng-ch'i-hsin-lun (大乘起信論)	1666
	Skt.	Mahāyānaśraddhotpāda-śāstra (?)	
63-V	*Ch.*	Na-hsien-pi-ch'iu-ching (那先比丘經)	1670
	Pāli	Milindapañhā	
64	*Ch.*	Ta-ch'eng-chi-p'u-sa-hsüeh-lun (大乘集菩薩學論)	1636
	Skt.	Śikṣāsamuccaya	
65	*Ch.*	Shih-mo-ho-yen-lun (釋摩訶衍論)	1688
66-I	*Ch.*	Pan-jo-po-lo-mi-to-hsin-ching-yu-tsan (般若波羅蜜多心經幽賛)	1710
66-II	*Ch.*	Kuan-wu-liang-shou-fo-ching-shu (觀無量壽佛經疏)	1753
66-III	*Ch.*	San-lun-hsüan-i (三論玄義)	1852
66-IV	*Ch.*	Chao-lun (肇論)	1858
67, 68	*Ch.*	Miao-fa-lien-hua-ching-hsüan-i (妙法蓮華經玄義)	1716
69	*Ch.*	Ta-ch'eng-hsüan-lun (大乘玄論)	1853

Vol. No.		Title	T. No.
70-I	*Ch.*	Hua-yen-i-ch'eng-chiao-i-fên-ch'i-chang (華嚴一乘教義分齊章)	1866
70-II	*Ch.*	Yüan-jên-lun (原人論)	1886
70-III	*Ch.*	Hsiu-hsi-chih-kuan-tso-ch'an-fa-yao (修習止觀坐禪法要)	1915
70-IV	*Ch.*	T'ien-t'ai-ssŭ-chiao-i (天台四教儀)	1931
71, 72	*Ch.*	Mo-ho-chih-kuan (摩訶止觀)	1911
73-I	*Ch.*	Kuo-ch'ing-pai-lu (國清百録)	1934
73-II	*Ch.*	Liu-tsu-ta-shih-fa-pao-t'an-ching (六祖大師法寶壇經)	2008
73-III	*Ch.*	Huang-po-shan-tuan-chi-ch'an-shih-ch'uan-hsin-fa-yao (黄檗山斷際禪師傳心法要)	2012A
73-IV	*Ch.*	Yung-chia-chêng-tao-ko (永嘉證道歌)	2014
74-I	*Ch.*	Chên-chou-lin-chi-hui-chao-ch'an-shih-wu-lu (鎭州臨濟慧照禪師語録)	1985
	Eng.	The Recorded Sayings of Linji (In Three Chan Classics)	
74-II	*Ch.*	Wu-mên-kuan (無門關)	2005
	Eng.	Wumen's Gate (In Three Chan Classics)	
74-III	*Ch.*	Hsin-hsin-ming (信心銘)	2010
	Eng.	The Faith-Mind Maxim (In Three Chan Classics)	
74-IV	*Ch.*	Ch'ih-hsiu-pai-chang-ch'ing-kuei (勅修百丈清規)	2025
75	*Ch.*	Fo-kuo-yüan-wu-ch'an-shih-pi-yen-lu (佛果圜悟禪師碧巖録)	2003
	Eng.	The Blue Cliff Record	
76-I	*Ch.*	I-pu-tsung-lun-lun (異部宗輪論)	2031
	Skt.	Samayabhedoparacanacakra	
76-II	*Ch.*	A-yü-wang-ching (阿育王經)	2043
	Skt.	Aśokarāja-sūtra (?)	
	Eng.	The Biographical Scripture of King Aśoka	

Vol. No.		Title	*T.* No.
76-III	*Ch.*	Ma-ming-p‘u-sa-ch‘uan （馬鳴菩薩傳）	2046
76-IV	*Ch.*	Lung-shu-p‘u-sa-ch‘uan （龍樹菩薩傳）	2047
76-V	*Ch.*	P‘o-sou-p‘an-tou-fa-shih-ch‘uan （婆藪槃豆法師傳）	2049
76-VI	*Ch.*	Pi-ch‘iu-ni-ch‘uan （比丘尼傳）	2063
76-VII	*Ch.*	Kao-sêng-fa-hsien-ch‘uan （高僧法顯傳）	2085
76-VIII	*Ch.*	Yu-fang-chi-ch’ao: T‘ang-ta-ho-shang-tung-chêng-ch‘uan（遊方記抄: 唐大和上東征傳）	2089-(7)
77	*Ch.*	Ta-t‘ang-ta-tz‘ŭ-ên-ssŭ-san-ts‘ang-fa-shih-ch‘uan （大唐大慈恩寺三藏法師傳）	2053
	Eng.	A Biography of the Tripiṭaka Master of the Great Ci’en Monastery of the Great Tang Dynasty	
78	*Ch.*	Kao-sêng-ch‘uan （高僧傳）	2059
79	*Ch.*	Ta-t‘ang-hsi-yü-chi （大唐西域記）	2087
	Eng.	The Great Tang Dynasty Record of the Western Regions	
80	*Ch.*	Hung-ming-chi （弘明集）	2102
81–92	*Ch.*	Fa-yüan-chu-lin （法苑珠林）	2122
93-I	*Ch.*	Nan-hai-chi-kuei-nei-fa-ch‘uan （南海寄歸内法傳）	2125
	Eng.	Buddhist Monastic Traditions of Southern Asia	
93-II	*Ch.*	Fan-yü-tsa-ming （梵語雑名）	2135
94-I	*Jp.*	Shō-man-gyō-gi-sho （勝鬘經義疏）	2185
94-II	*Jp.*	Yui-ma-kyō-gi-sho （維摩經義疏）	2186
95	*Jp.*	Hok-ke-gi-sho （法華義疏）	2187
96-I	*Jp.*	Han-nya-shin-gyō-hi-ken （般若心經秘鍵）	2203
96-II	*Jp.*	Dai-jō-hos-sō-ken-jin-shō （大乘法相研神章）	2309
96-III	*Jp.*	Kan-jin-kaku-mu-shō （觀心覺夢鈔）	2312

Vol. No.		Title	T. No.
97-I	*Jp.*	Ris-shū-kō-yō （律宗綱要）	2348
	Eng.	The Essentials of the Vinaya Tradition	
97-II	*Jp.*	Ten-dai-hok-ke-shū-gi-shū （天台法華宗義集）	2366
	Eng.	The Collected Teachings of the Tendai Lotus School	
97-III	*Jp.*	Ken-kai-ron （顯戒論）	2376
97-IV	*Jp.*	San-ge-gaku-shō-shiki （山家學生式）	2377
98-I	*Jp.*	Hi-zō-hō-yaku （秘藏寶鑰）	2426
98-II	*Jp.*	Ben-ken-mitsu-ni-kyō-ron （辨顯密二教論）	2427
98-III	*Jp.*	Soku-shin-jō-butsu-gi （即身成佛義）	2428
98-IV	*Jp.*	Shō-ji-jis-sō-gi （聲字實相義）	2429
98-V	*Jp.*	Un-ji-gi （吽字義）	2430
98-VI	*Jp.*	Go-rin-ku-ji-myō-hi-mitsu-shaku （五輪九字明秘密釋）	2514
98-VII	*Jp.*	Mitsu-gon-in-hotsu-ro-san-ge-mon （密嚴院發露懺悔文）	2527
98-VIII	*Jp.*	Kō-zen-go-koku-ron （興禪護國論）	2543
98-IX	*Jp.*	Fu-kan-za-zen-gi （普勧坐禪儀）	2580
99–103	*Jp.*	Shō-bō-gen-zō （正法眼藏）	2582
104-I	*Jp.*	Za-zen-yō-jin-ki （坐禪用心記）	2586
104-II	*Jp.*	Sen-chaku-hon-gan-nen-butsu-shū （選擇本願念佛集）	2608
	Eng.	Senchaku Hongan Nembutsu Shū	
104-III	*Jp.*	Ris-shō-an-koku-ron （立正安國論）	2688
104-IV	*Jp.*	Kai-moku-shō （開目抄）	2689
	Eng.	Kaimokushō or Liberation from Blindness	
104-V	*Jp.*	Kan-jin-hon-zon-shō （觀心本尊抄）	2692
104-VI	*Ch.*	Fu-mu-ên-chung-ching （父母恩重經）	2887

Vol. No.		Title	*T*. No.
105-I	*Jp.*	Ken-jō-do-shin-jitsu-kyō-gyō-shō-mon-rui (顯淨土眞實教行証文類)	2646
105-II	*Jp.*	Tan-ni-shō (歎異抄)	2661
	Eng.	Tannishō: Passages Deploring Deviations of Faith	
106-I	*Jp.*	Ren-nyo-shō-nin-o-fumi (蓮如上人御文)	2668
	Eng.	Rennyo Shōnin Ofumi: The Letters of Rennyo	
106-II	*Jp.*	Ō-jō-yō-shū (往生要集)	2682
107-I	*Jp.*	Has-shū-kō-yō (八宗綱要)	蔵外
	Eng.	The Essentials of the Eight Traditions	
107-II	*Jp.*	San-gō-shī-ki (三教指帰)	蔵外
107-III	*Jp.*	Map-pō-tō-myō-ki (末法燈明記)	蔵外
	Eng.	The Candle of the Latter Dharma	
107-IV	*Jp.*	Jū-shichi-jō-ken-pō (十七條憲法)	蔵外